STORIES FROM UKRAINE

The True Price of War

Bartosz Popko
Warsaw, Poland 2022
E-mail: 95booksproject@gmail.com

Printed Worldwide
First Printing 2022
First Edition 2022

ISBN: 978-83-966235-1-5 (paperback)
ISBN: 978-83-966235-2-2 (ebook)

10 9 8 7 6 5 4 3 2 1

Proofreading: Sara Lubratt
Cover design: Emir Orucevic
Introduction: Samantha Whaley

STORIES FROM
UKRAINE

TABLE OF CONTENTS

Introduction 1
Note from the Publisher 7
Prologue: Russia's War Through Different Eyes 9
Through the Eyes of Civilians 10
Through the Eyes of the Military 16
Through the Eyes of Volunteers 21
War and Dreams 27
We Are Not Underdogs 47
I Miss My Simple Life 59
Living in the Subway 73
Such an Unnatural Silence 87
Leaving a Country Behind 97
We Did Not Fall in Ninety-six Hours 107
This Is Not A Movie 119
Coming Home for the Fight 129
Life Under Russian Occupation 143
From Ukraine to Switzerland 153
Let Me Tell You Something 167
Sound of Missiles 191
There Is No Time for War 201
Silent Victims 209
My Inner Battle 221
Wake Up 231
If You Want to Help 249
Authors 253

INTRODUCTION

After two long years of enduring the COVID-19 pandemic, it finally seemed like things were beginning to improve. Then came the reports that a major conflict was brewing, and 2022 began with the prospect of a large-scale war in Europe. While Putin defended his deployment of tens of thousands of troops to the Ukrainian border as mere military exercises, governments worldwide were alarmed that the tactics could be a precursor to an invasion of Ukraine. By February 2022, there were as many as 190,000 Russian troops along the Russian-Ukrainian border, in Belarus, and in Russian-occupied Crimea.

On February 21, 2022, President Vladimir Putin gave a notable speech laying out a long list of grievances as justification for an upcoming "special military operation." In the speech, Putin recognized the independence of the self-proclaimed people's republics of Donetsk and Luhansk and ordered Russian peacekeepers into Ukrainian territory. Throughout Putin's time in office, Moscow has pursued a policy toward Ukraine predicated on the assumption that their respective national identities are artificial, and therefore fragile, requiring Russian influence and support in the region. This is far from true.

Russia had been supporting the separatist movements in these Ukrainian territories since 2014, but the new accusations and movement of troops marked a dramatic escalation. Following the increase of troops, Western leaders announced a new wave of sanctions. In the three months prior to the invasion, everyone argued about whether there would be a war and whether Vladimir Putin was bluffing. Some of the Russia experts who had long told people to take it easy were now telling them to be worried. Others, who had long criticized Putin, said that he was simply trying to draw attention to himself, that it was all for show. Putin had always been cautious—the sort of person who never started a fight he wasn't sure to win. But they were wrong.

In the days prior to the invasion, Ukrainian President Volodymyr Zelenskyy had made it clear that he did not want war. For better or worse, democracy was rooted deep in Ukrainian political culture. Still, the cultural and historical differences between the different regions of Ukraine would often surface in times of crisis. After the dissolution of the Soviet Union, Ukraine struggled to rebuild itself as a free country, but the people were determined and persevered through various political regime changes. As the years passed, Ukraine became stronger. In recent years, it has made enormous progress in consolidating a shared civic identity, making Ukrainian patriotism and national unity much more evident. Given the choice between fighting or surrendering to Russia, Ukraine has continuously decided to be a vision of change, resolved to fight for its right to freedom.

On the morning of February 24, Russian missiles hit military installations and civilian targets inside Ukraine, and Russian armored convoys crossed the border. Putin's unprovoked attack was condemned by leaders around the world. Ukrainians, seeing Russian armored vehicles coming at them, didn't freeze or back down. They didn't wait to be told what to do. They united. They acted. They fought back.

The evidence from the past few months suggests that Russian calculations turned out to be wrong. Ukrainian resistance has already far surpassed what Moscow was expecting. Russian forces have suffered tens of thousands of casualties and failed in their initial objective of marching on Kyiv. Today, more than five million Ukrainians have fled the country, and thousands more have been killed or wounded. Yet Russia has failed to achieve any of its stated military objectives and has itself suffered significant losses of both troops and *materiel*.

Despite the fact that they did not want the war to begin with, the Ukrainians rallied and persevered because through the chaos, anguish, and turmoil, they communicated what they saw, what they were doing, and what they needed. They figured out how to obtain essential supplies and equipment, how to solve problems, how to make things happen. They united as a nation, and they fought back.

The contributors to this book have each been given a chance to tell their story of what happened that fateful day as well as in the aftermath. The narrative covers events up until early October 2022. Each author has experienced this war firsthand and lived through the days that followed. They have all seen the destruction that war can cause. They have all felt the fear that comes with being in the middle of a war zone. They have all had to make split-second decisions that could mean life or death. And they have all had to live with the consequences of those decisions.

Readers will have a front-row seat to the events as they unfolded, through the eyes of those who lived it. These personal stories provide an intimate look at the human cost of war and remind us that behind every statistic is a real person with a story to tell. From interviews in the Ukrainian refugee camps, to a soldier on the front line, to families living in a subway, to broken dreams of successful professionals, to personal thoughts on how the war began, these are their stories. These are their memories of that calamitous day.

These are their thoughts and feelings about what happened and what it means for their country. They need to be heard.

NOTE FROM THE PUBLISHER

More than thirty people worked on this book. Most of them are Ukrainians.

The contributors to this book were given complete freedom to write whatever they wanted without any instructions or rules. Each opinion or political interest is expressed as the author's personal view. We made an effort to keep the individual authorial voices in the original style as much as possible, mainly correcting significant issues regarding diction or punctuation and making improvements to the flow of the stories. Therefore, some minor language errors may be found in the content.

The stories were written between August 2022 and October 2022. As you read this book, the war in Ukraine may be at a different stage, but the emotions and suffering of these people remain. Some characters' names have been changed to maintain their privacy and anonymity. The exceptions are persons whose first and last names appear.

Prologue: Russia's War Through Different Eyes

There was a power outage in the village, a rocket hit the neighbors' house. Later, the occupants started shelling the yard and outbuildings. They did not shoot at the house—maybe because they were adequate [sic]. But the neighboring family was shot dead.

This text was written by a local journalist. We managed to contact him through a branch of the press office in Poland.

Through the Eyes of Civilians

The third stage of the Russian-Ukrainian war began on February 24, 2022 with the entry of a column of Russian tanks into the territory of the Donetsk region at 3:40 a.m. and the invasion from the occupied Crimea at 4:00 a.m. It was a full-scale invasion. In the morning, the Russian offensives from other directions, in particular from Belarus, became known. Immediately after Vladimir Putin announced a "special military operation", Russian troops shelled dozens of peaceful Ukrainian cities. Just like that, without declaring war, while people were sleeping in their homes. Millions of Ukrainians woke up to the sound of Russian planes in the sky and rocket attacks. For many, this horror has been repeated every day for more than half a year, some were forced to leave their homes, and for some, a new day may never come. We've collected stories of ordinary Ukrainians about their lives during the war.

In Anticipation of War

"At 3:00 in the morning my daughter and I arrived by taxi at the Kyiv Boryspil airport—in about an hour and a half we had to board the plane to Egypt," Iryna from Kharkiv recalls this terrible day. "On February 23, in the morning, my husband and I sat down to breakfast in silence, because we understood that we had to make a decision—our intuition whispered to us that trouble would soon come. So we bought a ticket online for me and the child, first to Kyiv and then to Egypt. We decided that if the war, which everyone was talking about, doesn't start, we'd at least be able to relax at the sea. However, instead of the beaches of the Red Sea, we waited for long days on the road to the border with Poland, and then life away from home and husband. We didn't even have time to board the plane: all flights were canceled—the sky was closed, the war began. I don't even want to remember how we got to Lublin and then to Wroclaw. Probably every mother who evacuated with children in those days knows that it was a horror. Now we are safe, but it's not known when we will be able to return to Kharkiv, because Russians bomb it every day. The husband and his colleagues work in the office relocated to Ternopil. Our apartment in Kharkiv seems to be still intact, but I understand that at any moment we may not have a home, and this is a terrible feeling."

Life Under Occupation and Escape

Despite desperate resistance, Russian troops occupied and hold a part of the territories along offensive lines. In particular, Mariupol has been under occupation since February 28. The city, which in 2014 was captured—but not held—by separatists, with the help of Russians, was subjected to merciless bombing. According to Russia's plans, this 'strategic point' had to be captured at any cost. Many Mariupol residents were unable to leave the city in time and were forced to survive inhuman conditions. One of the residents of the city kept a diary from February 24th and later published it on Twitter, describing how communications and connection gradually began to disappear, how she had to live in the basement, and how she managed to leave the occupied territory. Below are some excerpts from her diary.

"Day 1: Woke up at 6:14... Started packing. First shelling of the airport, sirens... second shelling.

Day 4: The first explosion near us. In the evening the power went out. We spent the night at home in jackets.

Day 8: First day in the basement. The explosions are getting louder. It was so loud that my ears hurt.

Day 12: We decided whether to go to another place. We gathered under the shelling. On the way we prayed, everything was broken and on fire.

Day 14: Shelling of our area. They [*Russian military*] *were* just driving around and shooting at houses. It hit our garden. Only the door remained from the garage.

Day 17: There is not a single whole house left on the street and, apparently, in the whole city. Shells are flying, we are not even hiding anymore.

Day 22: People leave the city on foot—just to escape.

Day 26: Checkpoints happened constantly, cars were pushed to them to save fuel. There were a lot of broken vehicles on the way. When an APC and two tanks passed by, I thought it was the end. In Zaporizhzhia I restored everything on my phone and switched to Ukrainian."

According to the girl, she had to carefully prepare for the escape: hide all expensive things, sew money in underwear, "clean" and switch the phone to Russian.

Alina also shared her story from Mariupol. In the city, Alina and her husband had a good job, built and furnished a house, even managed to invite friends to visit in the spring. Her son, a fourth grader, was waiting for his graduation from primary school. The city itself had also developed significantly over the past few years. Now Alina and her son live in Germany, and her husband helps in Ukraine. Grateful for the shelter, the mother and son dream of returning to Ukrainian Mariupol. However, the city remains under the control of the occupiers, and the self-proclaimed authorities are in no hurry to restore it. The so-called aid is not enough, and those who could not leave are forced to live in ruins. At the end of August, it became known about 87,000 dead in the morgues of the city. This figure is not final, because many victims of Russian war criminals remain in mass graves, yards, parks, and under the rubble of destroyed buildings.

Refugees and Internally Displaced Persons

Because of the war, millions of Ukrainians were forced to go abroad, or as far away from the front as possible. At the beginning of the full-scale invasion, the regional centers of the western regions often worked at the limit of their capabilities, providing assistance to all in need. On his way to Poland, 15-year-old Ivan from Kyiv region stopped in Lviv for a short rest. The boy talks about how he dreamed of working as an agronomist, and how the Russian occupiers destroyed this dream.

"There was a power outage in the village, a rocket hit the neighbors' house. Later, the occupants started shelling the yard and outbuildings. They did not shoot at the house—maybe because they were adequate [sic]. But the neighboring family was shot dead."

Ivan's brother at that time was helping with humanitarian aid, his sister went abroad, and his father stayed at home with a rifle. The guy, like most refugees, had a long way ahead. In the early days of the war, people waited in line at the border for days—without supplies, in the cold, uncertain about the future. Children were sick, frightened adults were even more exhausted. Volunteers came to help: Ukrainians, Poles, citizens of other neighboring countries. Everyone tried to provide the necessary assistance. Generators were brought to the checkpoints, heated tents and lighting were installed. A lot of help came from Poland, including clothes and food.

Strong Because We Are United

Deadly missiles, endless military equipment, and more than two hundred thousand occupants did not make Ukrainians surrender. Today, everyone is doing everything possible to speed up the victory, and many refugees have already managed to return to their homeland. Having organized themselves, the people of Ukraine defend their freedom. We tell real stories of people to support this struggle and counteract the hostile Russian propaganda.

Through the Eyes of the Military

On February 24, the whole of Ukraine was under the gun of the Russian army. The invasion came from the territory of the Republic of Belarus, the Russian Federation, the occupied part of the Luhansk region, as well as from the occupied Crimea. Thus, the front line stretched for 2500 km. On the first day of the war, the Russian occupiers took control of the Chornobyl nuclear power plant, including the exclusion zone. In the south, Russians shelled and captured Zmeinyi Island, approached Kherson and Melitopol. Simultaneously, there were attacks on the eastern and northeastern directions. Ukrainians were forced to act: to take up arms, to negotiate in an emergency mode with suppliers of equipment, machinery and weapons, to go to safe places.

Army and Mobilization

The Ukrainian military have performed a miraculous feat, stopping a Russian army of thousands and convoys of military equipment several kilometers long, continuing to do so for over six months. Maksym, an officer of the Armed Forces of Ukraine from Lviv, says that the most difficult thing was to prepare the military for the reality they would have to deal with. However, already at the front, despite constant shelling and exhausting battles, Maksym's unit repels the aggressor.

"There are wounded, but most of them will return soon. We are confident that sooner or later we will be able to defeat the enemy. At some point the Russians will run out of equipment, and without it they will not be able to do anything."

Among the Ukrainian military there are many volunteers from different regions of Ukraine, of different ages and professions. Some joined the army immediately, others joined the Territorial Defense Forces. In the occupied regions of Ukraine and Crimea, a rather large-scale guerrilla resistance movement immediately unfolded. Collecting stories of the military is a real professional challenge for journalists, because talking to the press is usually the last thing they want to do now, during the war. Despite this, we managed to talk to some of the Ukrainian heroes.

Roman is a history teacher, journalist, and after February 24, a volunteer and combatant in the Territorial Defense Forces. On March 2, Roman began preparing to perform tasks in the combat zone. Like most of his comrades, the man had no military experience, but this did not stop him from fulfilling his duty.

"At first, we trained at the training ground. After that, we were sent to Donetsk region. It was hard to overcome fear, but even harder to lose friends and comrades. Many good fighters were killed," the serviceman said.

During the war, Roman's old leg injury was aggravated, and he had to take painkillers, eventually returning for treatment. However, not only the military but also ordinary Ukrainians are killed and injured. The terrible events in Bucha, Irpin, Mariupol and other occupied cities and villages of Ukraine claim the lives of tens of thousands of civilians. And the Russian policy of destruction of the Ukrainian language and culture, combined with propaganda, has reached catastrophic proportions.

"Everyone sees that this is genocide, that Putin wants to destroy Ukraine. Therefore, we have no other choice but to win," Roman concludes.

Ukrainian Heroes

Despite the invincibility and high morale of Ukrainian soldiers, the war takes lives. In May, 100 Ukrainian soldiers were killed in one day. On August 22, Valeriy Zaluzhny, Commander-in-Chief of the Armed Forces of Ukraine, reported about almost 9,000 fallen heroes. Widow Olena tells about her husband, "cyborg" Vladyslav.

"We had a lot of plans. Vlad's contract was about to expire. After February 24, he came home for the first time in June. Shortly after his departure, we celebrated the birthday of our daughter, 7 years old. Vlad called, congratulated me... But he never saw the photos from the holiday that I sent him. It was hard to hold back tears, I cried and screamed. My daughter immediately understood everything, started to calm me down..."

Olena did not believe in the death of her husband until the moment she was given his wedding ring. The younger daughter of the hero celebrated her first birthday on her father's grave.

Not only men risk their lives for the victory of Ukraine. Today, more than 57,000 women serve in the Armed Forces together with volunteers of territorial communities, almost 32,000 of whom are in the combat zone. Ukrainian media regularly tell the stories of women warriors to the public. These are, in particular, the ICTV Facts project, which collected the stories of 12 military girls, the TSN project "Women in the Armed Forces: Ukrainian beauties who took up arms and 'poured' to the occupiers", as well as the special project of the Ukrainian edition of ELLE "Women at the Front".

"I come from a military family. My father is at the front now, and I have been a career serviceman since 2014, when Russia launched military aggression against our country," says Svitlana from Ivano-Frankivsk. "The first loss of my friends shocked me and I also rushed to the front in 2014. Although we can say that the war for me began with the Maidan, because among the Heavenly Hundred is my close friend... Now I am defending Ukraine in one of the brigades of the

Ukrainian army. Ukrainian women do a lot for our victory not only at the front, but also in the rear, and only together can we defeat the enemy!"

"Ukrainian women are not only victims of war. They are fighting on all fronts along with men," First Lady of Ukraine Olena Zelenska said in an interview with the media of the Republic of Korea. And this once again proves to the world that Ukraine is a modern country with democratic values, for which Ukrainians are ready to fight to the last drop of blood, to victory.

Through the Eyes of Volunteers

On February 24th, Ukrainians woke up with an understanding of the need to unite and help the Armed Forces of Ukraine for victory. The wave of volunteering began with donations to the army, and later covered humanitarian issues. The initiative was joined by Ukrainians abroad, temporarily displaced persons, ordinary citizens from different parts of the world and entire states. Very quickly, the Ukrainian volunteer movement spread all over the world, as assistance to Ukraine became a symbol of the struggle for freedom and human values. In this article, we have collected stories of people who are engaged in volunteer activities at different levels and help Ukrainians bring victory closer.

Volunteer Movement

The volunteer movement gained large scale support in Ukraine back in 2014-2015. Then the revolution of Dignity had just ended, Russia occupied Crimea and launched an invasion of the Donbas, and resources were very limited. In response to these challenges, a circle of people formed who became volunteers to provide the military with equipment, weapons and other necessities.

After February 24, 2022, there was a kind of revival and scaling of this movement, in accordance with the number of mobilized military personnel and the pressing threat. Nikita

Perezichny, now the head of the NGO "Voda", says that he had never volunteered before and did not plan to do so. However, the war adjusted his plans.

"I have a friend at the front. I once offered to help him with the equipment, but he wrote that he had everything, and sent the contacts of another military man who needed it. And already from him and his commander I received a list for half a million hryvnias. The joint efforts of friends managed to raise part of the amount, but it was obvious that for such purposes it was necessary to increase the reach. This is how our organization was created. We try to fulfill smaller requests, which large funds—such as "Come Back Alive" or The Foundation of Sergey Prytula—do not cover. In the first month of the war, there were many requests for equipment. Bulletproof vests from Europe had to be bought more expensively, and, for example, mittens could be of worse quality, but at that time it was better than nothing. The issues of thermal imagers and night vision devices are always relevant."

For half a year, Nikita became convinced that Ukrainians are ready to help each other even in such difficult conditions.

Another aspect of volunteering is helping civilians. Andrey—a fitness trainer from Kiev, a father and a volunteer with experience—took the family abroad, and returned to help the residents of the Kiev region. Under the shelling, a volunteer and his friends carried food, supplies, and took people out.

"On March 5, we came under fire, and after it we were all surrounded. But, fortunately, the Marines came to the rescue. We were quickly taken out, so it cost only six lost cars, a friend's leg injury and other minor injuries. The next day, we continued to evacuate. It's a pity that it's impossible to help everyone."

United for Victory

According to a survey conducted by Ilko Kucheriv's "Democratic Initiatives" Foundation, 57% of Ukrainians from the center and west of the country have joined volunteering or charity, while 11% still plan to do so. Ukrainians are engaged in volunteer activities both within the framework of initiatives of companies and organizations in which they work, and outside of work. "In the beginning, our team united spontaneously. On weekends, two colleagues and I regularly took food and medicine to Kharkiv, and on weekdays we collected money among friends and colleagues, bought and packed the necessary things. Finding fuel wasn't easy at the time, so we never knew if we could go with help on Saturday or not. But in most cases, we found a solution," says Alexey, an employee of a Kiev IT company.

"From the very beginning, my team and I decided to help with what we can do best—feed people," Irina, the owner of a restaurant in Chernihiv, shares. "So we started cooking regularly for the local Territorial defense. There was a period when there were enough funds, but there were problems with the logistics of products. When the products ran out, our customers and friends came to the rescue, as well as people who had read about our initiative on social networks. Therefore, when, for example, the grandmother of our bartender Igor gave us cabbage and sugar from her own stocks so that we could feed our defenders, it was clear that we could not be defeated, because every Ukrainian does everything and even more to support the military."

When Russian missiles from the Black Sea began to hit Odesa, 38-year-old Ekaterina and her two teenage sons left for Germany. "I lost my job in the first days of the war, so I had plenty of time to volunteer," she says. "I coordinated the purchase of necessary things for military personnel through my sister, who lives near Cologne. There was an urgent need for various equipment—from bulletproof vests to shoes. We handed over the purchased items to the military on the Southern Front in the Kherson and Mykolaiv regions. When the rocket attacks became very frequent and my sons and I decided to go to my sister's house, I already understood what I would do in Germany. Now I continue to coordinate the purchase of necessary things, a list which we receive from our brothers on the front."

Charity Foundations

From February 24 to June 30, 2022, 4,365 civil society organizations were registered in Ukraine (according to the Center for democracy and the rule of law (CEDEM), received from the Ministry of Justice of Ukraine). Among them are charitable foundations of various scales, which were joined not only by professional fundraisers, but also by people for whom such work has become a new experience. Large Ukrainian businesses initiated the creation of their own funds, while medium and small businesses joined the large funds that were formed before and during the full-scale war. The state, for its part, adapted a number of laws to develop the activities of non-profit organizations. So, for example, if a volunteer receives compensation for travel expenses or medical examinations, this money is not considered their income. Accordingly, the volunteer does not pay taxes on them—personal income tax and ERU. The same applies to training in pre-medical care, psychological adaptation, or working with PTSD.

To be sure that your donations will actually be received by volunteers and sent to help those who need it, you should listen to basic advice and transfer funds only to trusted volunteer organizations that have official accounts with the

National Bank. Transparent foundations control the process of purchasing, receiving and transferring equipment/ assistance, collect and store all acts and documents, publicly report on their work, and post photo and video reports. You can find the necessary information and view reports on official websites and social media pages.

During the six months of Russia's war against Ukraine, a number of foundations have been formed that have earned the trust of both Ukrainians and foreign benefactors. Among them are the above-mentioned foundation for competent assistance to the army "Come back alive" and The Foundation of Sergey Prytula, as well as United 24, KSE Foundation, Kolo, Future for Ukraine and many others.

Though victory depends on many factors, the motivation and unity of Ukrainians and the whole world certainly help to bring closer the day when peace will come to Ukraine.

War and Dreams

War, oddly enough, leads not only to catastrophic consequences. To some extent, we can even thank it for some things. For the fact that we become completely new people and discover new facets and skills in ourselves.

Taras Romashchenko Ph.D

War is about ugly deaths, horrific injuries, unimaginable suffering, numerous destructions, but not only. It is also about the destruction of the most cherished or everyday dreams of those who are killed, as well as of those who, despite all the horrors and challenges of war, eventually survive.

Before Russia's unprovoked full-scale attack on Ukraine in February 2022, each of millions of Ukrainians had their own dreams and aspirations. The author of these lines also had them, but the war made its insurmountable adjustments to the plans. However, first things first...

When guns speak, science will wait!

Have you ever thought about what an ambitious scientist and, at the same time, a teacher dreams of in modern Ukraine? Probably everyone who is involved in the academic sphere in our country will have their own answer to this question. Someone will put in the first place a noticeable increase in wages as a necessary material basis for future professional achievements. And he will be right, because, unfortunately, during all the years of independence, the attitude of the state to scientific and pedagogical staff in this matter leaves much to be desired. For some, the priority is the opportunity to work fruitfully with indifferent or, if lucky, gifted students, to pass on their knowledge every day and see how future professionals are being formed before your eyes—talented managers, engineers, economists, doctors, programmers, and other specialists in their field.

At the same time, I am convinced that, answering this question, there will be many who associate their ambitions in the scientific and pedagogical field primarily with the possibility of constant and comprehensive professional growth and self-improvement. Scientists (teachers) are undoubtedly creative people. And true creativity, as you know, does not recognize any restrictions, and strives for new challenges and horizons. To achieve such horizons in the field of academic life allows, among other things, cooperation with representatives of foreign scientific circles—like-minded people from leading universities or institutes of Europe and the world.

I belong to the latter category, especially about international cooperation in academic and other spheres. There are several logical explanations and, if you like, prerequisites for this. First, there were diplomas with honors on obtaining higher education as a specialist in Romance and Germanic philology. That is, English and German are not native languages for me, but very close and every day, especially the first one. Suffice it to say that at the university for foreign students I teach specialized economic disciplines in English, for many of whom this language is native.

Your humble servant was not limited to higher education and soon decided to radically expand his professional profile. As a result, he continued his postgraduate studies, after which he successfully defended his PhD thesis in the specialty—World Economy and International Economic Relations.

Having become a PhD in Economics (equivalent to a Doctor of Philosophy in Economics in the Western world), who also speaks foreign languages, I was actively involved not only in the process of direct teaching at the university, but also found myself in the vortex of international scientific life. Regular participation and speeches abroad at international conferences, seminars, and forums; organization of lectures with prominent foreign scientists at the university; holding round tables for Ukrainian students and teachers with the participation of representatives of foreign universities and international organizations—this is not a complete list of my professional activities. The latter were dictated both by my own aspirations and initiatives, and by a new responsible position at my university—Deputy Director of the Educational and Research Institute of Economics and Law for International and Image Activities.

I was able to successfully combine my love for foreign languages, my own scientific interests in the field of international economics and official duties at the university, at my institute (faculty). However, I was not going to stop there. The next stage in my personal professional growth was to be a qualitatively new access to the international arena through the European grant system for Ukrainian scientists and teachers.

For those who are far from this topic, it should be emphasized that winning a grant or funding for your own research project or topic is not an easy thing. This is true even if it is the domestic, Ukrainian market. Much more difficult are the prospects for winning European Union grant programs. For most of my colleagues, this is an almost impossible task, especially when it comes to social (not exact) sciences, which include international economics. However, is this a reason to give up? Obviously, no! And I did not give up...

In order to find and enlist the support of a supervisor at a well-known foreign university, to exemplarily substantiate the topic of your own research, to find independent reviewers of the project and to prepare several supporting documents, it would seem an impossible mission. Almost impossible... Over the past few years, there have been several such attempts on my part, and finally, in the summer of 2021, I received a coveted letter stating that, having passed the sieve of meticulous selection, I finally achieved my goal—I received a grant to conduct research at one of the prestigious Austrian universities. During the whole semester, I will be able to exchange experience with leading scholars in the field of globalization of migration processes and explore the peculiarities of investment activities of diaspora representatives in the countries of origin.

After a short euphoria came the realization that life would soon change radically. And there was so much to do, namely: to finish all the affairs at the university, to obtain a work visa to Austria (unfortunately, the Ukrainian biometric passport does not allow a long visa-free stay in the European Union), to rent a house, to develop a route and buy tickets to the destination. And most importantly—before a long separation, to enjoy the home comforts of the family in the circle of his beloved wife and two little heroes. The eldest son was seven, and the younger one was not yet one year old. I coped well with all the tasks because there were six months left before the start of the grant. Now the count is down to the bottom. All the suitcases are packed, the last instructions are given, which means that their father is ready to fly towards science in the EU!

But this dream was not destined to come true. There was a date on the plane ticket to Vienna: March 1, 2022. Four days before, the first missiles exploded in Ukraine and the impossible in the XXI century became a reality. A great war came to Europe when the demonized Russia decided to destroy my homeland.

And then there was the war...

I remember in detail the 24th of February this year. It was not yet 6 o'clock in the morning when my mother's phone call woke me up: "Son, the war has started! Rockets are exploding all over Ukraine." And then there were the first tears, many tears...

As best as I could, I reassured my mother, promising that everything would be fine (who could have known about the scale of the tragedy that was coming to all of us, Ukrainians?!) and passed out. I quietly got up and dressed so as not to wake my wife and children. My thoughts were surprisingly clear and concrete: "Drinking water, necessary food, cash from ATM."

It immediately became clear to me when I went outside that hundreds and thousands of other Ukrainians received similar calls this morning. It seemed that it was not six in the morning, but lunchtime on a holiday—so many people were around. In the convenience store, there were long queues, empty shelves, noise, excited conversations and... tears again. Including the sellers who had to be at work, but their hearts ached and broke for those who stayed at home.

Having bought everything I needed, I went to the ATM. In vain. The queue to it was measured by dozens, if not hundreds, of people. I had no desire and, frankly speaking, no time to wait. I really wanted to hug and embrace my family. In addition, it was not known whether there would be enough cash for everyone. I suspect that about halfway through the queue, the ATM was empty, and some people left with nothing. After thinking about it for a minute, I turned around and went home, from time to time looking at the sky and searching for missiles with my eyes.

At home, my family had already got up and were surprised to meet their father from somewhere at such an early hour. My wife took the news that we had been attacked by Russia and a real war had begun calmly, probably believing in herself and hoping that all this was some terrible mistake, and it could not be true. As for the children, due to their age, they did not care. And thank God! The younger one was crawling on the floor either in search of his toys or the feet of his loving mother. The older one was preparing for lessons at school, which, of course, did not exist that day.

So, in the family circle, the first day of the full-scale war passed. Ahead were months of horrible crimes by Russia against Ukraine, whose dreams of a peaceful and prosperous life were crushed by the newly emerged fascists from the East.

War in messengers

The first weeks of the war changed everything. There was no memory of the former peaceful life. Ukraine plunged into events that it had not seen since the middle of the XX century, when the Second World War raged and devastated all life on its territory. I could tell a lot about those incredible horrors that Russian invaders brought to our land. About the destroyed, burnt to the last brick Ukrainian towns and villages, about the brutal murders of pregnant women and babies, about the rape and torture of thousands of my fellow citizens, about the looting of everything that comes to hand, as well as about the incredible spirit and heroic resistance of the entire Ukrainian society to the Russian invasion. Resistance unexpected by the world! However, why do it? I think you, dear readers, know everything perfectly well and see it every day virtually live. Thanks to the Internet.

Instead, I would like to say a few words about how the war, its first days and weeks, affected me personally in psychological terms. I am not a very emotional person. To be more precise, sometimes I can be overwhelmed with emotions, but usually I keep them tightly inside. Only in exceptional cases can I let them out. War once again confirmed this feature for me. I did not let out all my feelings about what is happening in Ukraine. Until I was forced to do so...

From the first days of the Russian attack, I did what I had to do. Mostly it was about meeting the needs of my family. There was enough time for this because my teaching at the university suddenly stopped. Universities, schools, kindergartens, businesses, organizations, and other institutions—everything was closed. The country stopped.

The streets were empty because all people, except for the military and those connected with the security sphere of the country, tried to stay at home at the first opportunity. Even during the day, not only at night, when the curfew came.

And at home, in addition to household chores, there was and, thank God, still is the Internet. I tried to spend every free minute during the first few days after February 24 on my smartphone. I did not have such a habit before, but the war and the free time that suddenly appeared changed everything. Channels of live news from the front started working on popular messengers and the whole country began to read, re-read, share comments, etc.

I have become a regular reader of such modern media. And in my case, this passion became too obsessive. I could read one channel for hours, switch to the second or third, and then return to the first one again and again in a circle. The amount of information from the front line, which was published literally every minute in messengers, was so great that sometimes I spent whole days and nights reading. It suited me, because in this way I was completely immersed in myself with my hidden experiences. I immersed myself not for the sake of emotions as such (they were completely different—from indescribable despair to restrained optimism), but for the sake of reading something that would give me hope... Hope that Ukraine will stand and will not fall on its knees before the "second army of the world", as Russians used to call themselves.

However, the medal, as you know, has two sides. If I was satisfied with this situation with virtual isolation, my relatives were not so much. To put it mildly. Especially my wife. She was frankly and rightly annoyed by my immersion in the Internet. She tried to get me out of there by talking about how life goes on and everything will be fine again soon, and I, when I emerged from the virtual world, was angry with her (here I partially gave free rein to my emotions) and pointed out her shortsightedness. Like, don't you understand—there is a real war and nothing else matters! You need to be aware of the events!

However, my wife with her feminine wisdom was right. You cannot focus only on the negative. It can drive you crazy! Today, seven and a half months after the outbreak of the war, I understand this very well, as well as how wrong I was in those early days with such an excessive enthusiasm for messengers and news in them. My awareness of the events taking place at the fronts sometimes did not add confidence to the family, but, on the contrary, frightened my loved ones. For my inappropriate behavior from the pages of this story I want to apologize—sorry, my family!

Returning to those first days, I must admit that about two weeks after the start of the war, the messengers were gradually finished. No, not quite, because I still regularly look through them, but that strange fanaticism is no longer there and will not be. And I am very glad about that.

Family safety is above all!

From the first moments of the war, one fundamental thought settled in my head, the head of father and husband. Another, a new dream, if you will. From the very beginning of hostilities, I was clearly aware that everything was very, very serious. Unfortunately, as my wife convinced me (she really wanted to believe in it), it will not end quickly and there is no guarantee that Russian boots will not set foot on the ground of my city in the heart of Ukraine. At the first stage of the war, everything was going to the fact that my regional center would also be occupied. How could there be other thoughts if the invaders bombed the capital itself—the millennial Kyiv? From Kyiv to my native Cherkasy, it is 180 kilometers to the south or two and a half hours by car.

Realizing the real danger, I calculated the options where and how, if necessary, I could evacuate my wife and sons. There were a lot of options. The scientific world, as it turned out, is very friendly. In fact, immediately after the outbreak of war, I began to receive letters and inquiries from my foreign colleagues and friends: how are you, how can we help you, can you somehow get to the western border, and we will meet you and take you to a safe place? There were really many such offers. The geography was impressive: from Austria and Poland to Germany and the USA. Truly, friends in need are friends... Thank you again for your concern!

While there were no theoretical problems with the potential destination (there was plenty to choose from), the road was not so simple, or rather very difficult. The first months of the war were a total collapse on the roads and railways. The former was complicated by numerous checkpoints, and therefore, it would seem, a normal and short trip turned into a dangerous and very long journey, because it was forbidden to move at night during the curfew. According to the experience of a friend who evacuated his family by car, it took almost three days to get to the border. And this is even though in peacetime, a similar journey took about 10-12 hours. As for trains, evacuation routes for women and children were soon launched by the authorities, but it was almost impossible to get on them. There were several hundred seats on each train, but several thousands of people wanted to get on. It is difficult to describe in words what was happening at the stations and platforms in those days. And I have small children. My youngest son, as I mentioned above, was not even a year old at that time. He would not have been able to withstand such a journey in the arms of a standing mother (trains were overcrowded and people often could not even sit down). And for the older ones it would be a real challenge. It is unlikely that at the age of seven a child can be ready for something like that.

There was one more difficulty: my wife did not want to leave me, a person liable for military service, alone. Yes—it was scary, yes—sometimes something small exploded somewhere nearby, but due to the remoteness from the main fronts, our city was relatively safe. She insisted: "I will not go abroad without you!" And no matter how I persuaded her, she stood firm. Apparently, her position would have remained so until now if everything had remained unchanged in terms of security.

However, it did not happen as expected. The first terrible explosions near our house happened somewhere in the middle of spring. It was our military who shot down missiles flying near the city in the direction of Kyiv and fell into the Dnipro River near us. I will never forget the expression on the face of my eldest son, who ran up to me with tears in his eyes and said: "Dad, I don't want to die!" For a father, this is the worst thing his child can say. And for my wife, as it turned out, it was a turning point. The next day she came to me and with the confidence of a mother, ready for anything, said: "Send us somewhere—the children must be saved."

I did not have to be persuaded. The plan for such a case had long been ready in my head. A letter to Germany, a short correspondence with a professor I know, an official invitation for an internship at his university (my wife is also a teacher) and in two and a half weeks I was alone at home. Like in a famous Hollywood movie. By the way, when my wife and children were leaving by train, the situation was much better. Yes, the journey was not easy for them, but at least everyone had their own place in the carriage.

Being left alone, I realized the bitter irony of life: a researcher of international migration processes, became an indirect participant in them, having sent abroad the most precious thing he has—his family.

The war shattered another dream of mine—to be with my younger son when he makes his first independent step in life. Without holding hands with his parents...

War is not a hindrance to education

My work at the university practically did not stop. Yes, there was a period at the beginning of the war when there were no lectures and seminars for three weeks. However, the teaching process gradually resumed. Considering the force majeure circumstances, the university management decided to provide online education for those students who had such an opportunity both in terms of security and psychological conditions, as well as in terms of physical capabilities. The fact is that many students also evacuated from Ukraine or became internally displaced persons, and therefore did not have constant access to the Internet.

In the classroom from the very first day we, teachers, have done and are doing everything to support students. We teach educational material, but we also try to inspire with our words faith in the future of Ukraine, its victory over the ruthless enemy. In my opinion, it is very important that students understand that life goes on. And even despite the war in the country, their dreams of modern education will come true! No one has given up and everyone is doing their job in good faith on the ground: the military—on the front line, and the teacher—in front of students at the university.

Starting this fall, the management of the educational institution went even further. I would even say, at some risk. It was decided to conduct combined classes: both offline and online. If there are students who want to be present in the university classroom, the teacher should work offline. The students were divided into two groups. Some (they are the minority, but they are there) attend the university, others stay at home. For a teacher, this is a challenge and some inconvenience, because you must tear yourself away, giving a lecture or conducting a seminar at the same time for those who are sitting in front of you in the classroom, and for those who are looking at you from computer screens. However, we do not complain much. You are conducting a seminar and suddenly an air raid alarm sound. You calmly stop the online meeting, gather all the students in the classroom and lead them to the bomb shelter. After the alarm is over, you return to the classroom and continue the educational process. Such times...

During the ongoing war, I did not forget about my scientific interests and international cooperation. Moreover, I try to regularly inform foreign colleagues about what is happening in Ukraine, about migration processes involving Ukrainian refugees. To this end, I have repeatedly held online meetings and made presentations to scientists from leading Austrian, Canadian, Polish, German, and other Western universities. During such conferences, the gratitude of foreign colleagues to all Ukrainians who defend not only their independence, but also the independence of other democratic states is especially impressive. They all pay tribute to the incredible bravery and, without exaggeration, legendary feat of Ukrainians.

Contribution to the victory

Ukrainian people are unique in their own way. No matter how different, contradictory, and even irreconcilable we may sometimes be in ordinary, peaceful life, in times of trouble all Ukrainians unite into a single organism and work side by side for a single goal. Today everyone does what he can do on the way to victory. A successful man leaves his lucrative business and goes to the front line as a volunteer, a student-programmer joins the ranks of cyber troops, an old grandmother bakes pies and sends them through volunteers to the front line, and a grandfather displaced from Donbas goes every day to weave protective nets for the Ukrainian army. And there are thousands of such examples!

What do I personally do to win? The usual things. I transfer money to the army, collect money for a car for the front, buy food for territorial defense, send the necessary clothes, conduct an active information campaign against the invaders on the Internet, etc. Recently, I also learned about the opportunity to help the Ukrainian army in a new financial way—to buy military bonds (a novelty from our government). As a result, I became the owner of three dozen such bonds. Is this total contribution enough? Let everyone decide for themselves. I just told the truth.

Although not all of them... There are several bomb shelters at the university, where city residents come to hide during air raids. Male teachers of the university ensure the operation of such bomb shelters. It is a round-the-clock duty for the safety of citizens. Our task is to meet and accommodate people, to report suspicious persons, as well as to ensure that order and safety are maintained on the territory of the educational institution during such duties.

Unexpected "gifts" of war

War, oddly enough, leads not only to catastrophic consequences. To some extent, we can even thank it for some things. For the fact that we become completely new people and discover new facets and skills in ourselves. For example, I am a pretty good cook: I am not a stranger in the kitchen, and I can do a lot of things in it. However, there are dishes that only my wife pampered me with, and before her—my mother and grandmother. For example, we can talk about the world-famous Ukrainian borscht.

Now that my wife and mother are abroad (and my grandmother will soon be in heaven), borscht is gone. But I still want it! As it turns out, a strong desire, first-hand recipes, and a trip to the store for the right ingredients work wonders. My borscht is no worse, and maybe even a little better than my women's. Because it is mine! In general, when you are suddenly left alone, you must do a lot of things that others used to do for you. The division of labor in the household has disappeared, and therefore there is an objective need for self-improvement. I am not against such an upgrade.

But the main thing that the war has led to is the emergence of new dreams. So to speak, it took away the old ones in exchange for new ones. I have such aspirations now: to survive, to see and hug my wife and children again, as well as to wait for victory. Millions of Ukrainians, for whom the war with Russian barbarians has become a truly national one, aspire to the latter. Such wars are not lost!

October 7, 2022.

Taras Romashchenko Ph.D, Associate Professor
Department of Economics and International Economic Relations Institute of Economics and Law (Deputy Head)
Bohdan Khmelnytsky National University of Cherkasy

We Are Not Underdogs

I wondered what would have happened if that missile had fallen first. What would have happened to me if there had been a mistake? Would I have become a "civilian victim," one of the many Ukrainian victims since the beginning of the conflict?

Roman K.

When I am asked what I can say about the war in Ukraine, I immediately become silent. On the one hand, there would be too many things to say, and indeed, a whole book would not be enough to tell everything. On the other hand, I live in western Ukraine, and I have never experienced the war firsthand. Lviv, the city where I live, has never really been invaded, and I have not seen the cruelties that took place in the east and north of my country.

Despite all the difficulties, I could still tell the stories that I experienced, and to do so, I cannot help but go back to February 23, 2022, and remember it all from the beginning.

At that time in Lviv, one could feel what I call "war air." I remember it very well because that strange feeling, similar to the calm before the storm, could be felt everywhere in the center.

On the evening of February 23, walking in the streets, looking at people, then with friends. We went to the pub for a beer. I could relax without feeling nervous, which became normal after a while.

I remember we argued for a long time about what would or would not happen, and we all came to the same conclusion: Putin probably was not crazy enough to invade. It was not convenient for him to do so, and more importantly, he could not really expect to win. None of us believed that he would misjudge the Ukrainians, and we all, in short, thought that nothing would happen. We were sure those two hundred thousand troops deployed around Ukraine were probably just another bluff.

So, we went home a little relieved, happy to realize we were right and thought that everything the next day would be as before. Life would go on as if nothing had happened.

And yet…

I was awakened at 7:30 a.m. on February 24 by my mother, who told me about the war in a trembling voice. I immediately felt the adrenaline rising in my lungs. It was mixed with disbelief. How was this possible? Why had this happened? Was this really happening all around me?

I realized there was no time to think. The count was running out. Something had to be done because the news from the east was disastrous. The Russians seemed to be advancing everywhere, and if they continued like this, Ukraine would soon cease to exist.

However, in those first hours after the invasion, I also understood that this would not happen because the hatred for the Russians was such that their attack would soon turn into an all-out rout. It could not have been otherwise. We would not fall, and in a short time, I thought I would find myself fighting them. Of course, it frightened me. I was not a soldier and had never had any military training. But hatred was speaking for me. Hate combined with fear, but hate nonetheless.

I waited for a couple of hours before a military store opened. I wanted to buy my own uniform, shoes, gloves, and everything else I would need during the cold days of February. Finally, I announced my intentions to my family and left.

The first thing that surprised me was the inevitable panic of people. There were huge queues in front of the pharmacies. The supermarkets were now completely empty. In fear, people were trying to buy basic necessities, such as water, bread, and medicines. Helicopters flew overhead. Ambulances could be heard in the distance.

Yet, in that surreal atmosphere, there was an unusual feeling of intensified solidarity. It was not that it had not been there before, but it had increased that morning. I saw it everywhere. It was as if everyone wanted to do their part, like helping an old lady cross the street or giving up their place in line to a pregnant woman. Unlike what I might have expected, no one was trying to climb over the others. No one was trying to get away. No one was complaining. There was both panic and fear, but they were constructive feelings. What really mattered was helping each other.

This vision cheered me up, and when I was on the bus to the military store, I knew that we would not fall. There was not the slightest chance that this invasion would succeed. They would not prevail. My thought was confirmed a little later when I arrived at the store.

It was now empty.

Within thirty minutes of its opening, there was nothing left. I barely managed to combine the military trousers, similar to the English uniform, with the army jacket, identical to the Spanish uniform. There were no shoes in my size, so I chose ones one size bigger.

Satisfied with the choices I made, I brought everything to the counter. Here came the first problem: The Internet was compromised, so I could not pay, and the seller asked only for payment in cash. The banks had virtually instantaneously banned using credit cards to make purchases up to a certain amount, and I did not even have a banknote on me. So I asked to put that stuff aside, and convinced that I would withdraw cash from an ATM, I left.

However, I had not reckoned with the situation. By 10.00 a.m., almost all the ATMs in the neighborhood had been emptied. I could no longer withdraw the money, and another dilemma arose: What should I do?

I returned home disgruntled, waiting to see what the news would be. It was shaping up to be a hot week and realizing I could not stay away, I started looking for other solutions.

At first, I went to the recruiting office, but when I arrived in front of the building, I saw a line of men there that was, to say the least, immense. There were people of all ages, and despite the initial terror and the sad news, there was a feeling almost as if we were all going to a football match. You could feel a particular fighting spirit decorated with a few jokes here and there.

In short, we were excited about facing the greatest danger of our lives.

Of course, the tension could be felt despite the smiles. Everyone knew it would be hell, but everyone was willing and happy to endure it despite the Russian army's terrible reputation.

The unusual temperatures on February 24 only seemed to make us stronger. It was uncommon on those wintry days, but it was also encouraging. We stood in line, convinced that we would do everything we could to protect our country. And then… and then… they told us there were too many of us. We could not all serve in the army because they could never equip us. There were not enough uniforms. There were not enough rifles. And they could never train us.

So when they told us to come back tomorrow and added that there were too many of us, I knew I had to wait a bit, but again, I did not reckon with the various contingencies.

I went home desolate and said I would try the next day, but when I went to the recruiting office again on February 25, I saw that the line had grown even longer. So, I began to ask people how long they were standing in that queue, and I found out that on February 25, many had already arrived from the eastern and northern regions. Some men had fled from Bucha, Irpin, and Ukraine's central areas. They had fled from those lands, but they immediately tried to enlist once they arrived in Lviv. However, I never found out whether they had succeeded, because after standing in line for another couple of hours, I realized that there would be nothing left to be done. I could have stayed there another three to four more days; but in the end, they probably would not have taken me anyway.

So, I decided to go a different way.

When I returned home, I first decided to quit both of the jobs I was working. It was clear that I could not continue working with this situation in Ukraine. So, I communicated my decision to those in charge (at that time, I did not know that I would remain unemployed for a while) and started looking for volunteer battalions.

I knew they were taking pretty much everyone. Or, at least, that was the case in 2014 when Ukraine faced another crisis. Of course, these battalions were detached from the official military. They were different. A bit dangerous, but at the same time, I already knew that they were professional. Many volunteer battalions were composed of specialized people who had a lot of experience behind them and could get all the necessary weapons.

But would they equip me? Would they train me? Would I be needed?

Curious to learn and ready to go, I immediately started calling. The first number was busy. The second, the same. On the third, they asked me if I had served in the army, and when I said no, they said they would call me back. So, I called the first number again, which was still busy.

Not happy with the results of my efforts and not understanding how this was possible, I tried to contact them in other ways. I tried writing to their email address. I went to their Facebook page and wrote to them there, but I got no response.

It seemed that getting into the volunteer battalions would be much more complicated than in 2014, when several of my friends managed to enlist. Incidentally, in 2022, those who had enrolled in 2014 did not manage to enlist either for a simple reason: there were too many volunteers and too little equipment. For this reason, the first official criteria were created. Only those with no health problems, those who had done their military service, and those with some experience behind them could join the army.

With nothing left for me to do but wait, I already knew that I would probably never be called up. I had no military service and I had slight health problems, so I would be a last resort.

What is more, the clouds on the horizon seemed to be clearing.

The first positive news was beginning to come from the front. The Ukrainian army seemed to have pushed the Russians back from Hostomel Airport. Encouraging news was also coming in from the other sides. In short, not only did the situation not seem as pessimistic as we thought it would be, but as I had guessed, it had begun to turn positive. That belief that we would hold out and that Ukraine would certainly not disappear was strengthened. We were not underdogs at all; we were underestimated.

And we should have proved it to the world. We were the masters of the situation, and we should have made that clear to everyone. I, for my part, would have done my best to make that happen.

Not having a job, I dedicated myself entirely to helping others. I started unloading vans with humanitarian aid from

Europe. While waiting to be called into the army or a volunteer battalion, I did everything I could to help others, and it was an experience that changed me. At that time, Lviv had become a gathering point for people fleeing from all over Ukraine. Some people had lost everything: family, jobs, pets. There were those who, frightened and terrified, wanted to escape to Poland, Germany, or Austria. In a short time, Lviv had to deal with an unbelievable number of people, to say the least.

And then came the first bombings.

I first heard a missile pass over my head on March 26. I lived (and still live) not far from a factory that repairs tanks, and that day, the factory was hit by Russian missiles and severely damaged.

I remember it as if it were yesterday. Their whistles passed over my apartment building. I heard how they cut the air, and then I listened to the roar. The windows in my house shook. I also felt a particular fear. But then again, I should have gone to the shelter, which I did not. There were so many bombings and sirens that we got tired of running for cover after a while. We preferred to stay at home, aware of the danger.

I will never forget that feeling. It was the first time since February 24 that my life was in danger. I wondered what would have happened if that missile had fallen first. What would have happened to me if there had been a mistake? Would I have become a "civilian victim," one of the many Ukrainian victims since the beginning of the conflict?

I also noticed people's reactions. Sure, there was a particular fear, but on the other hand, I saw that those bombings had not "broken" them morally. None of them would have preferred to submit to Russia to avoid being bombed. They would have chosen, instead, to live freely as Ukrainian citizens, despite all the dangers coming from the east.

Of course, we were bombed at other times as well. We frequently heard the siren; missiles were coming from Belarus, the Caspian Sea, and the Black Sea. However, after a while, even that sound, which was supposed to warn us of danger, became "normal." It became part of a strange daily routine.

It did not scare us anymore.

Just as we were not afraid of that invasion, the more days that passed, the more we understood that the Russians had gotten themselves into a bigger problem, and they would not get out without suffering monstrous losses. Patriotic feelings only grew. I already knew they would never take Kyiv. I also knew that we would eventually turn the tide of war. It was inevitable. It was understandable. It was a fact.

Then, even the war became a normal situation. I continued to do what was necessary, but the news of the fighting did not worry me as much as it did at the beginning. By the end of April, the situation had returned to normal, and it was clear that they would lose. Everyone tried to get back to doing their own thing as much as possible. With time, the flow of refugees also stabilized. Lviv continued to be an important center in this respect, but many other cities in western Ukraine also began to take in more people.

Meanwhile, many preferred to return to their homes in April, when the situation was still not entirely secure. Fortunately, the Russians did not have enough strength, and they would not invade the Kyiv area again. It seemed that the Russian danger was now over.

I am still waiting to be called up, but I suppose that time will never come again. Besides, the situation on the front seems optimistic, and the war, with those tragic events of February 24, looks a long way off. Of course, anything is possible. But it seems that now there is more need for people behind the front line rather than on the front itself. Everyone, therefore, is doing their own thing, waiting for that longed-for victory that will certainly come.

Our victory, after all, is only a matter of time.

I Miss My Simple Life

Strangely enough, our son slept soundly. I did not want to wake him up. I guess I wanted to prolong the last few hours of his peaceful life. This little four-year-old should not have known what war is. Children all over Ukraine should not know the words bomb, missile, fighter jet, enemy, war, and many others at such a young age. I did not know what to do.

Yana Rybak

Waiting for death is worse than death itself.

If anyone wants to know what it is like to live in anticipation of war after it has started, read this letter.

I have the simplest family: a husband and a little son. The three of us lived, and worked; the child went to kindergarten for the first time in September 2021.

Everything was fine; everything was like it was for everyone else. A simple life, plans for a new home and a car, dinners with the family, entertainment for the child on weekends.

I learned about what Ukraine could expect by accident. In January 2022, on social media, I saw an appeal from our President that he would do everything possible to ensure that every family in Ukraine celebrated Victory Day in the same way and had a peaceful spring. And then I was filled with different emotions. Fear for our future, faith in our country, and hope for peace.

I cried. It was the first time I had cried after hearing the news. As it turned out, it was not the last time. Overcome with anxiety, I realized we cannot irresponsibly treat the threat that hangs over our country. I decided we must prepare everything the three of us need and pack it in a small suitcase, which we will take with us in case of danger.

For a person who lived in peace and security, it is hard to imagine how you can put your whole life in one suitcase. But our family was not the only one who did it. Just three days before Russia invaded Ukraine, I ordered drinking water, stocked up on food, and was prepared.

I was discussing with my friend how things might develop. She and her husband were about to leave for Poland to change their lives. She did not have time.

I hoped until the last moment that everything would work out. After all, this is the 21st century. We live in a time of civilized countries where diplomacy is not the last word. Never in my life could I imagine that I would have to live through a war.

I am not complaining. Compared to other people in Ukraine, I am lucky. I did not hide my child in creepy old basements. I did not have to share the last of my food and water with other adults and children. My family and I were not in the territory occupied by Russia. But this does not mean that such people, many of who are still in Ukraine, have not experienced these aspects of war. Our psyche is broken. Life will never be the same again.

It is hard to believe, but we Ukrainians dream of very simple things.

I dream of going to work every day. I dream of drinking coffee in my apartment in the evening, sitting by the window, unafraid that a rocket will hit our yard. That my body will be cut by the fragments of the same window. I dream of walking around the city at night. I want no one and nothing to limit my freedom. I dream of just walking with my son on the playground in my hometown.

Unfortunately, Kharkiv, where I lived for the last 15 years, has become very dangerous for my family. And this is not the fault of Ukraine. It is the fault of that country, which in the modern world decided is superior to others. This country, like in primitive societies, decided to conquer territories. It decided to turn another nation, another culture, into slaves. And for seven months now, no one can stop it.

Back in 2014, when Russia annexed Ukrainian Crimea, I could not believe that it would get away with it so easily. I am a lawyer. For me, law and international law are not empty words. For Russia, they are empty.

The last week before the attack, I was depressed. I was not happy about anything. I just wanted this situation to be resolved as soon as possible. But certainly not by war. Even then, I felt the need for the fastest possible development of events. The uncertainty was killing me. My state, and, I am sure, the state of all Ukrainians, was very similar to the one we found ourselves in after February 24, 2022. Russia had ruined our lives even before that. Before that, it was able to launch its tentacles into our world. But the night of the invasion is a night none of us will forget.

February 24, 2022

Strangely enough, I still don't believe it happened. This night, around 5 am, we woke up to explosions. I now understand they were not as close to our house as it seemed. But do you know how loud bombs sound from several kilometers away? This sound is enough to wake up sleeping people with their windows closed. This sound could not be confused with anything else. Somewhere in the depths of our souls, we felt there was hope. We wanted to believe that it was some other sound. But we knew what it was. From that moment, you can safely divide your life into before and after. With the bomb explosion, our peaceful life ended, and an aimless existence began.

My husband panicked. He thought we should urgently take our small suitcase and go to the shelter. However, I was afraid to be on the street, a child in my arms with rockets and bombs flying over me.

Strangely enough, our son slept soundly. I did not want to wake him up. I guess I wanted to prolong the last few hours of his peaceful life. This little four-year-old should not have known what war is. Children all over Ukraine should not know the words bomb, missile, fighter jet, enemy, war, and many others at such a young age. I did not know what to do.

I just waited. I waited for someone to tell us what we should do, where to run, and whether we should wait for something. We hoped that there would be no long war. We hoped that everything would settle within a few days, and we stayed home.

A lot of people left. In the first hours, those who had a car left. We did not have time to buy one. The next days, the railway was overcrowded. The remaining people tried to escape by train. We stayed at home.

The family we were friends with went to their relatives in another region. This region does not border Russia, so it was considered relatively safe. Still, we stayed at home.

We did not go out or walk outside for 10 days. On the first days, I went out in search of food. Everyone knew that no one would bring food to the supermarkets anymore. People would no longer stand in the markets to sell food. Almost all the pharmacies were closed. I was counting on the food stocks I compiled earlier.

I wanted to stay at home until the last minute, in my walls, where I feel comfortable, which somehow also made me feel safe. But my husband convinced me to leave. He believed that our city could be surrounded, we would not be able to leave, and we would face starvation. Looking at my little son, I decided that I had to leave my past life and take him to a safe place.

Why run away?

We fled to another region, closer to the center of Ukraine. We hoped that Russian troops would not be able to get there so quickly. We could only observe the situation. Millions of Ukrainians went abroad in search of safety. They took their children. I wanted to stay close to my husband. It could have had numerous consequences, but we had to support each other at that moment. I was offered assistance in leaving many times. Each time, the doubt killed me, but every time, I stayed close. I told my son we may have to leave his father and go to another country. He immediately said he did not want to go without his father. My eyes were bursting with tears.

After leaving Kharkiv, I realized we did the right thing. We were able to go outside with our child again, buy him a ball, and play football with him. He had almost no toys of his own because there was absolutely no space in the suitcases. But we were together. Unfortunately, Russia got there too. It launched its missiles all over Ukraine. No matter where you were, you were always in danger.

Now I understand that one of the most important and valuable human rights is the right to life. No one dares to violate it. A sense of security is a guarantee of your tomorrow. You can make plans, you can hope, you can strive for a goal, and, most importantly, you can live. Anyone who takes away your security has no right to exist.

My parent's house, where I spent all my childhood, fell under occupation. There was no communication with my hometown for many months. People from there could not leave for territory still controlled by Ukraine. We knew little about the people who stayed there. Since the local authorities cooperated with the occupiers, the town remained intact. Today, we know that people there do not have the basic benefits of civilization: water, electricity and gas. People survive by cooking over a fire. Food is not delivered there. How long they can live in these conditions remains a mystery. We pray only for the speedy liberation of these territories by the troops of Ukraine. Only then will people be saved.

That is why it was worth fleeing the territories threatened with occupation in the first place. Life there would have become impossible.

Life without goals and plans.

We are now seven months into the war. You may ask how our life has changed during this time.

Radically. It is completely different. And most likely, it will never be the same. I do not know what people felt during the Second World War, but for some reason, it seems to me, something similar to what we are feeling now. Our life is now a constant expectation of victory. We believe that good will win. After all, this is exactly what we were told in childhood fairy tales. Why, then, does humanity exist if anyone who considers himself stronger can step in and crush a weaker opponent, stealing everything from him?

I can no longer make plans. I have no purpose because I do not know if I will be alive tomorrow.

My every day starts and ends with the news. I don't know whether I should say thank you, or vice versa, regret the existence of social networks and the Internet. But this is the main source of information about the front. And it is the main source of a good or bad mood each day.

Not so long ago, the Armed Forces of Ukraine liberated a large territory in the Kharkiv region. This was one of the greatest achievements of Ukraine during the war so far. Of course, it increased our morale, rooted in faith in victory. Many now hope that Russia will shell Kharkiv less. But I don’t think that’s true. This insatiable beast will bite off a piece of our life until its last day.

Recently, the defenders of Azovstal returned to Ukraine. It is impossible not to cry watching the video of their meeting with their families. How can there be so much grief in the world? And all this grief was created by a single person.

He has brought too much pain and loss to people in Ukraine. We cannot respect him. We consider him stupid. He is the result of unchanged power for more than 20 years.

He is an egoist. He does not think about any homeland; he thinks only of himself. He wants to go down in history. He wants people to talk about him, and he wants to be remembered. But everyone will only dance at his funeral.

Video of the first shots of the liberated territories, Bucha, Izium... I could not stop crying. Hands fall. I cannot believe that this is possible in this world. Why are there people who can bring death, abuse, pain, and grief? These people do not repent. They do not believe that they did something wrong. They do not consider themselves guilty. And I feel powerless.

I understand that this man will not allow himself to lose. He is like Hitler. He would rather shoot himself than admit defeat. He will bite into Ukraine until he can no longer. He will use all the weapons he has to win.

I am afraid of nuclear war. I do not want to see this terrible spectacle. I do not want to cope with it. It seems to me that even if I am not in the epicenter, my heart just can't stand it. And he continues to threaten the world.

I don't know what's next. This is the biggest problem. A person who does not know what he lives for cannot build his future. It seems to me that during these six months, I have grown gray hair, which I shouldn't have seen for another 20 years.

Every evening, my husband and I listen to political scientists. It is very interesting to know what smart people think about the new circumstances of the war. But the problem is that their opinions are completely different, and no one knows what will happen next. Only one person knows.

I cry every day. I, the girl who was more cheerful than others at her job. Who surrounded herself with happiness and joy. I can't laugh anymore. I don't know if you will understand, and I would not understand this myself. At least not me that existed before February 24, 2022.

It's very hard. It's like you're always waiting.

I don't remember my life before the war. It's strange, yes. But I remember that it was wonderful. Whatever we lived then, it was a happy life. Now we all know that we lived well. And we would have continued to live like that if not for the war.

Many of my friends ended up abroad. This is a side effect of the war; it destroyed all social ties. Relatives are scattered all over Ukraine. Some remained in the occupied territory. I have lost communication with some of them. Someone stayed in a basement in Mariupol for more than a month.

And do you think any of them know what to do next? No, they do not.

My friends have been in Germany for six months. They still have no permanent housing. They have no job. If you were a successful lawyer here in Ukraine, you are a nobody outside of it. And no, no one is afraid of hard work. But to get it, you also have to deal with a lot of competition.

Everyone is very grateful to the world that supported and sheltered us. But the vast majority of people who left want to return home. They had everything here: home, work, and friends. Everything was broken. They were not allowed to choose.

It is one thing when you believe that you will be better off elsewhere and want to live and work permanently in another country, but it is another when you are forced to put your life in one suitcase and go somewhere, no matter where. Just imagine it for yourself. What would you do?

I listen to our President every night. I believe him; I want to believe him. The whole country is hoping for victory. We believe in it. Sooner or later, but sooner is better. Every day takes many lives. Every day children lose their fathers or mothers, or both at once. Someone loses their children. None of this would have happened if Russia had not attacked.

And we call it a war. Not a special military operation, not a conflict, not just an invasion, but a war. If this is not war, then what? What else should happen? What does war look like then?

It is strange to me that 140 million people in Russia tolerate this. And it is even more surprising that many of them support the war. How? How is that possible? You read the same fairy tales as we do. You watched the same movies and live in the same world. Why do you want to destroy it? Why don't you stop it? It's a pity. It is a pity that many people have no will. They just don't value freedom. Neither theirs nor anyone else's. They are slaves.

Today, cities near which there are no hostilities live... They just live. There are buses full of people, supermarkets with lots of food, and somewhere you can even watch a movie. But all this does not bring pleasure. Believe me, it does not bring pleasure to any of us.

The greatest pleasure will be to celebrate the victory. To celebrate the New Year in my apartment. In my hometown, with all my friends, and, most importantly, my lively family.

Our President, giving another interview, said these words with which 100% of Ukrainians will agree. Russia can leave, but Ukrainians have nowhere to go, we have only this home.

My God, when will it all end?

P.S.

To whom is this letter addressed? I don't know. Perhaps to someone for whom a person and his life mean something. Perhaps a child who could grow up to be the next dictator, but after reading this, will grow up to be a normal person.

Maybe for someone who does not even know where Ukraine is. Or for someone who will think that nothing special happened a few years after the victory. Or maybe someone, after reading this, will dare to fight for themselves and their rights in another country to prevent the usurpation of power. But, in general, for those who will benefit from this letter. And may there never be war in your home. This is the worst thing that can happen.

Living in the Subway

Some of my other friends had been in the school bomb shelter since the beginning of the war. It was very hard—it was cramped, there were many people, and they had to find ways to walk their dogs.

Elena St.

It started with a call from my friend at 6 a.m. on February 24. I worked that night almost until the morning (I am a freelancer, and a night schedule is part of my everyday life), so at 6 a.m., I was still sleeping. I did not understand why Vika (my friend) was calling so early, and I was afraid that something had happened to her. And she asked: "Are you all right? Haven't you heard anything? Kharkiv is being bombed."

I didn't understand what it meant—bombing? A couple of minutes later, I heard explosions on the street. I called my friends, and we decided to go to the subway. My son was sleeping all this time; the explosions I heard did not sound close, so I decided not to wake him up until it was clear what was happening.

I remember standing in the middle of the room and not knowing what to do, what to take with me, and how it happened that war came to Ukraine. Finally, I decided to wake up my son, explaining that we had to go to the subway (it was a 10-minute walk from my house), and we got ready, put our cat in a carrier, and left. In the subway, we met our friends—children and their parents who we normally went with to developmental circles. It was so strange. There we were with our things, and people around us were going about their business as if nothing were happening. I felt like I was in a dream. We spent a couple of hours there in the subway and then returned home that day, because the children needed to eat and go to the toilet, and the adults needed to cook something. And, as it turned out, to take with us more necessary things, like warm clothes, blankets, and food that could be stored for a long time.

In the subway

The next day, the bombing became louder, so we gathered in the subway again. That day, there were already many people at the station. They were arranging their lives as they could—some had tents, some had air mattresses, and some just sat on blankets. People did not fully understand what was happening, everyone was scared, and no one knew what to do or expect.

My son, cat, and I were lucky—at the beginning, we managed to take a more-or-less cozy corner, protected by walls on two sides. As a result, there was almost no draft. Those who came later had to settle right on the stairs because the entire platform was so busy that there was only a narrow passage on each side.

At night (that is, during the curfew), the entrances to the subway were closed with special metal shields. The children liked to watch how they opened and closed. If permission was given by the subway management, the shields were opened at 6 a.m. each day.

After a few days, we developed a routine: when the shields opened, we quickly ran home to bathe, then my son undressed and slept in his bed, and I ran to prepare a couple of days' worth of food, just in case. Then I would feed my son hot soup and run back to the subway. Sometimes, while my son was sleeping, I went to the store to buy groceries. At that point, there were already interruptions in the supply chain. Frightened people were buying everything regardless of the price. And I was frightened, too, after standing in line for a couple of hours under fire (it was very scary not for myself but for my son—what would he do if I did not return?), so I bought everything we could possibly eat.

Once a shell fell somewhere close enough, and the whole crowd of people that were in the upper part of the station ran down. It was terrifying, and I am still grateful that my son and I were in the corner and the crowd did not knock us down, because otherwise who knows what would have happened?

My son found new friends in the subway, boys of the same age, and they played together. My parents and I agreed to take turns watching the children: someone watched while the others ran upstairs to buy something. Somehow I was lucky enough to get to the pet store, where there was almost no queue, since the saleswoman had just opened the door. I stocked up on food and litter for our poor cat, who had been with us all this time in the subway and sat frightened in the carrier or stayed at home. I was turning gray thinking that if a rocket hit our house, the poor animal would die. But in the subway, he could not eat, drink, or go to the litter box—the unfamiliar surroundings and crowds of people scared him very much. At the same time, this intelligent animal very quickly understood what was what, and when we started to pack, he would run into the carrier, close the door behind him with his paw, and look out with large, frightened eyes as if to say, You will not leave me here alone, right?

While we were in the subway, I saw that many other people had taken their pets with them: there were cats, dogs, parrots, and even a guinea pig.

People in the subway quickly got to know each other and started to help each other, which was great. Our neighbors were a lovely couple of pensioners who looked after our things while I was running home with my son. Now that woman is in the Czech Republic. She went with her daughter, but her husband stayed in Kharkiv.

A few days later, some of our friends decided to go to the region, to the village. Of course, we were apprehensive about them getting there safely because the roads were being shelled, and traveling there was a gamble. But, thank God, they arrived, and now they are also in the village. My friend's husband is a military man, and she and their daughter will not leave him.

Some of my other friends had been in the school bomb shelter since the beginning of the war. It was very hard—it was cramped, there were many people, and they had to find ways to walk their dogs. They also stayed in Ukraine; first they went to Western Ukraine, then to Poland, but then returned and are now in Kharkiv.

At first, life in the subway was chaotic and disorganized, but after a couple of days, everything started to get better. Volunteers brought food and goodies for children, but also cardboard, foam, and mattresses. These were distributed to people who had nothing to sit or lie on. We lived on the outskirts of the city, so there were no trains at our station. But closer to the center, there was a train with a checkerboard pattern on one side, and people arranged their homes in the cars—I saw it later.

This time was probably most challenging for mothers with newborn babies. Although some rooms were allocated for them, the subway is the subway, so they were not able to wash, to bathe their children, to clean their clothes… even boiling a bottle was a quest. And when the pharmacies closed and there were no diapers or formula in the stores, it was a nightmare.

I realized that something had to be done, that it would not end, and I could not risk my son's life or health. My work colleague had taken his family to a remote village and said I could come too—there would be housing and food. But it did not seem to be an acceptable option for me, as I'd be somewhere in the countryside, without a car, with a child, in the midst of a war. I am a city person and used to having all the necessary infrastructure nearby, so I did not go. I was just afraid that I would not be able to cope with the situation if something happened.

At the end of the first week of the war, people gradually began saying that we should flee abroad. I had never been abroad in my life, and such a thought seemed completely wild to me. How would it be to just leave everything and go somewhere else? Besides, they said that there was absolute horror at the train stations. It was impossible to get a train, the station was filled with wounded people, and the trains were being shelled. But running back and forth under fire with a child and a cat in a carrier was also scary.

The deciding factor for us was the soldiers in our yard. One morning, we ran home as usual, and I was cooking in the kitchen. Then I saw through the window that armed soldiers in uniform were moving around the yard. I was so confused. I could not tell whether they were orcs (Russians), and I should quickly pour boiling water on them from the window, or they were ours. I ran to my neighbor for help. He had served, and when he saw their uniforms, he knew they were ours. But for me, it was the last straw; my child could not stay in a place where soldiers were shooting. And when I woke up the next morning, I realized we must leave. Immediately.

My son and I came home one final time. I chose some comfortable clothes, packed our documents, some food, water, and cat food and litter, tucked my sweater into the cat carrier so that the cat would not be so scared, dropped the keys off to my neighbor, and we left our house for the last time.

My neighbors, who we'd seen every day and then lived with in the subway, also left. They went to their relatives in Western Ukraine and now live there. One neighbor stayed at home. I left her the keys to my house as well as a fridge full of food (because I, with my unpredictable nature, bought a lot of food, medicines, and other necessary items and then the next day decided to leave) and all the things that were left at home. I still cannot take them, so I may as well let someone else use them.

Fleeing to the train station

The train station was about 40 minutes away by public transport or car. But they were shooting, and no one knew where bullets would fly next time. So I decided to go through the subway tunnel—it was not scary, and relatively safe. Quite a lot of people were walking that way, leaving the stations in groups and walking together. We also went with a group who helped to carry the cat and our bags part of the way, but we still quickly fell behind, because my little son could not walk as fast as the adults. So as we walked alone, we sang songs and recalled all the rhymes he learned in kindergarten. I tried not to let my son perceive this transition as an escape but just an unusual little walk. People walking towards us said that the station was a complete horror, that there were many wounded and crippled adults and children, and that there were fights breaking out among those trying to board the trains. Many people, upon seeing this, went back, but not us. I felt that we must go forward, break through, and leave, because otherwise, it would be impossible to survive here. I decided that if everything was as scary as I'd heard at the station, I would cover my son's eyes with a scarf and carry him in my arms so that he would not see, but we would pass no matter what. My son is a real hero. At age six, he boldly walked along the track in front of me, did not whimper, and did not ask to stop or turn back. He just went forward. Just in case, I told him several times that if something terrible or incomprehensible happened, he should run ahead as fast as possible, and at the station, he should find the duty officer and ask for help. Even before going into the tunnel, I wrote many small notes with my son's data (his name, surname, age, address, and contact phone number) and put these notes in all the pockets of his clothes.

That day we could not get to the train station; we simply ran out of energy and had to spend the night at the subway station, which was separated from our destination by only two crossings. Some people found us a place in a subway car, fed us, and gave us a blanket. It was very warm there, my son slept comfortably, and I let the cat out at night to walk around the car. Like a small child, the cat sniffed and looked at everything around him with huge, surprised eyes. Everything was new and exciting to him.

The following day I found out that the subway management had banned the passage through the tunnels. They said too many people were walking through. It was terrible news, as we had not yet reached the train station. Walking along the streets with a child and a cat, I knew we would be perfect shooting targets. But some friends of friends found people who helped others like us to evacuate, and they took us to the train station by car. When we finally emerged from the subway, I did not recognize what I saw: all the small shops were smashed and looted, and piles of spent shell casings littered the ground. It was so scary. As we made our way to the station, they started shooting, and explosions were heard very close. At the station, I saw many Ukrainian soldiers, tense, with weapons in their hands.

We went to the platform where the evacuation train was boarding. It was already filled with more than enough passengers. But we were again lucky. Just then, another train arrived at the same platform but on a different track. At first, people rushed to get on, and I saw that we would not be able to fit in with the cat carrier. I told my son that we would wait for another train because I would not leave the cat. Luckily, a policeman heard me. He looked over at us, then pushed the crowd of adults aside a bit, helped my son into the carriage first, I followed, and he handed me the carrier with the cat. I hope this man is alive and well, because he saved us all that day.

There were seven of us in the compartment: my son and me, another mother with two daughters, a girl, and a woman. So many people were on the train that it was almost impossible to walk down the corridor to the toilet. It turned out that I was the only one in our compartment who had water, so we divided what I had between everyone. We had traveled for a long time when we passed Kyiv. At that point, all the lights went off and the train stood there for a long time. It seemed to me that a Russian missile could arrive at any moment, and that would be it. We would be gone. My son woke up and started to cry. He wanted to go to the toilet, but between the blackout and the people sleeping in the corridor, it was impossible to pass. The cat, who was in his carrier under the seat, started meowing. He was also frightened. I was kneeling in front of the seat, stroking his head with one hand through the carrier's door and calming my son to sleep further with the other, trying to convince both of them that everything would be fine. That night my whole life passed before my eyes—so many lost opportunities, unsaid words, and so many things I did not have time for.

Thank God, we traveled that dangerous stretch without incident. About 30 hours after we left Kharkiv, we arrived in Lviv, and from there we reached the border with Poland by car. On the train, we'd had a little snack in the morning, but on the road, there was no time. My brave little son did not whine and did not complain. Only once, just before we reached the border, he cried because his stomach hurt. It was not surprising—he'd been hungry for more than a day, a cold and nervous child who had walked half the city and did not understand what was happening.

We stood at the border from about 6:00 p.m. to 12:00 a.m. We left Ukraine on the 5th of March, although because of the time zone change, when we arrived in Poland the next day, it was the 4th of March. Once in Poland, we were met with hot tea and scarves. Right after the crossing point, on the way to the buses, many volunteers gave people hot tea, coffee, and soup. We hadn't had anything to drink or eat for more than a day, and that tea was an absolute miracle. There was also a box filled with warm hats and scarves for us to take. I could hardly believe that you could go up and take a scarf, just like that.

We took a bus to Przemyśl in Poland and finally were able to rest. And in the morning, we started a completely different life. My family was safe, and this was the most important thing.

I thank God that everyone I have been able to contact is alive and well. I hope it will continue to be so. My colleague lived in Saltivka, and a shell hit his apartment, but he and his family were already far away in the countryside. My friend, who lived not so far from us in Kharkiv, is now in Norway. My son's little friend from developmental classes, along with her mother, are in Germany.

My son was supposed to have graduated from kindergarten this year and start first grade in September. But unfortunately, all this was taken away from us by the war, and all the children from his kindergarten class are now in different countries. My son misses his home, his friends, and his whole life. I am also very sad and angry. I hate the occupiers and still cannot understand—how is it possible that in the twenty-first century, in a civilized world, they are killing children and civilians, and for what? Why? And when will it finally stop?

I am overwhelmingly grateful to Poland for everything—shelter, support, and all the help we received here. We came here because Poland was one of the few countries that accepted unchipped pets then. That was essential for me, because our cat had a passport and all vaccinations, but I did not have time to make a chip for him.

We arrived in dirty clothes, without any things at all, because there was no question about whether to choose our clothes or the cat. Of course, I chose the cat. And people helped us so much that now we have everything we need to live. We will never forget it, and we will always be grateful to Poland and the Polish people.

Such an Unnatural Silence

I remember standing in the kitchen, cooking, and then I heard a whistle, a very loud whistle. My brain immediately recognized that the whistle was a rocket. I screamed. I remember that everyone ran into the corridor.

Anna B.

On the night of February 24, my boyfriend and I woke up to the alarm and a call from my roommate. She said in a very excited voice, "Anna, the war has started, wake up…" and the call ended.

After her words, we were shocked, but we instantly forgot. At first, I felt that it was all a dream and not true. I was skeptical about the news of Russia's possible outbreak of war because I believed in common sense. Because how can something like that happen in our time?

But no, as it turned out, common sense should have been rejected. Unfortunately, Russia does not have it.

So, let's go back to the morning of February 24. After my roommate's call, my boyfriend and I spent the hours until morning on our phones and computers, listening to the news, browsing various social networks, and reading all possible articles. We called our parents and relatives, talked to them, and stocked up on words of support and reassurance.

It was very awkward. Anxiety and a lot of thoughts were in the air. In the morning, my boyfriend's housemate came home from work. He was working the night shift, and he was terrified. He said that he heard some explosions and saw helicopters and noted that a long queue of cars had lined up to leave Kyiv.

From the window, we could see this line of cars, which remained for a day and a half. We systematically looked out the window at that line.

At that time, we saw everyone leaving, but we had nowhere to go because the apartment I rented with my friend was far outside Kyiv. It was not easy to leave Kyiv, and it was also hazardous, so we decided to stay at my boyfriend's house. The only thing was that my two cats were in my apartment. At that moment, they were safe with my friend. Then at 10:00 a.m., we gathered our thoughts, ensured that our neighborhood was safe, and quickly went to buy food because no one knew what would happen tomorrow.

We needed supplies. We did not have any at all. When we got to the store, we were shocked. None of us had seen such a queue, except in some historical photos from when people did not have enough food and it was issued selectively by coupons. We stood in line for a very long time, and when our turn came, there were almost no necessary products in the store. So, we decided to buy all that was available, including a few packages of six 1.5-liter water bottles because all the larger bottles were gone. Then we came home and started preparing some food for a couple of days, and my friend called me again.

She said that because of stress and the fact that she was left alone at home, she decided to leave the cats and go from

Kyiv to Rivne, where her parents and relatives lived. She also said that she left food and water for the cats, and that was the end of our conversation.

From that moment on, my boyfriend and I started discussing how to leave the city and retrieve the animals sometime in the evening when there was no queue. We informed our parents that we had decided to take a taxi and go pick up the cats.

As we drove, fear filled the air. Each of us was thinking, "Just get there." While we were driving, explosions could be heard on the street; they were very far away, but still, they were pretty clearly heard. When we finally arrived, the planes flew so low that the house cracked, and the cats were hiding where they could. They were in shock. My boyfriend and I quickly gathered the cats, as well as all the documents we needed and everything that suddenly may be required, and ran back to the taxi car that waited all that time under the house (thank you very much!). We quickly got inside and promptly drove back. While we were returning to Kyiv, the taxi driver told us that he had transported many people with animals during the day and that he was not afraid of airplanes anymore. Therefore, he was very much diluting the anxious atmosphere while we drove. When we arrived home, we calmed and fed the animals and gathered some "anxiety bags," or essentials, just in case.

That same evening, my parents told me by phone that their city was shelled, so they were driving to their relatives in the village of Bobryk.

And then they disappeared.

The following days passed as if in a fog, with constant monitoring of the news and the only desire that it all end as soon as possible. Every day, we could hear the shelling of the Kyiv region very well. It was very loud. After every explosion that was heard somewhere in the distance, we googled the information and understood that, yes, it was Brovary; yes, it was Bucha, and so on. It was scary.

From that moment on, we prepared a sleeping place in the corridor. But we decided to stay in the room for now. I do not know why we decided so. It was a very carefree decision on our part because every day, we could hear automatic gunfire and explosions. We were just in such a location where it was very well heard, and from the window, you could see the highway to leave Kyiv. Sometimes at night, we woke up from the thunderous noise of military vehicles moving somewhere in a line.

On February 26, the Beresteyskaya metro station, from which we lived two kilometers away, was shelled. It was terrifying and very loud, with explosions without interruption.

But it was even worse on March 1.

I remember standing in the kitchen, cooking, and then I heard a whistle, a very loud whistle. My brain immediately recognized that the whistle was a rocket. I screamed. I remember that everyone ran into the corridor. And when everyone was already in the hall, a loud explosion was heard so close to us. It later became known that the Russians hit the TV tower located two and a half kilometers from us. From that moment, the anxiety only increased.

Also later, the Lukyanivska metro station, which was located three kilometers away from us, was destroyed. It felt like we were living in a terrible dream.

The following days were like in the movie *Groundhog Day*. I lost my job. Later, my boyfriend lost his too. The days were so similar that we slowly began to get used to the atmosphere around us, which was probably very bad, but in this way, we were able to calm down and have less stress.

New anxiety was added to me through calls from my parents and relatives, who said that Russian troops had entered the village where they were all together. The town was occupied, and the Russian military was destroying everything in their path, raping women and looting houses around them. My family was lucky only because there were many of them, and they tried to stay in the house's basement most of the time.

Later, my mother called me and said that Russian soldiers had taken away their phones, except for my cousin's phone, which he had hidden in advance. My mother called from it. She also asked me not to call or write their numbers for safety. At the end of the conversation, we agreed that my relatives would call me only in the case of an emergency. And that was the end of our communication for some time.

The following days were disturbing. To distract myself, I started to study online with my boyfriend and on my own. Yes, maybe it was inappropriate. But we were distracted a little bit, at least. And we strongly believed in our military. We thought that eventually, our military would overcome the enemy, everything would stop, and we would need that education.

After some time, my boyfriend's neighbor came to visit his parents from Bucha, who were under occupation all that time.

My heart broke when I heard their stories. They were terrified and afraid of every rustle. They were afraid of the roar and even the creak of the door. It was so painful to watch. They also told us how the Russian military put them all in a group in the basement, and they were sitting there without food, water, or heat. And they were terrified when the Russians came and called some prisoners for a "conversation." Only women, elderly men, and children were left behind.

People were always afraid that they would be killed and their children orphaned or killed too.

They also said that the Russians made a fake green corridor and gathered people for executions at some point. And when they were going to the transport, they saw corpses lying in the yards.

When we were going to Kyiv, we heard from neighbors who had stayed in their homes about the atrocities committed by the Russians. Of course, their psyche was severely damaged. I felt their pain so much at that moment, and I understood their fears of different noises.

This fear was especially visible in the sister of a neighbor because she stayed with us for a while. One night, when everyone was already asleep, she heard a familiar explosion somewhere nearby. It scared her a lot; she immediately woke up, got out of bed very quickly, and with trembling hands, began to pack her things.

This also woke us all up. We went to calm her down, although we did not even know how best to do it. I will remember her reaction as a picture in my head for the rest of my life. I felt very sorry for her. Then she left us to visit her relatives abroad. I hope she is much calmer and better there now.

Then the days were like one again. Later, my parents contacted me and said they had left with their relatives through the green corridor back home. There were seven people together. There was also my uncle, who, despite all the persuasions of relatives, stayed in the village to feed the remaining cattle and guard the house against Russians, marauders, and dogs. My parents and relatives kept in touch with him until the complete liberation of the region.

I cannot remember the exact dates, but eventually, the Ukrainian military liberated the Kyiv region from the occupiers. When it was almost calm, my boyfriend and I decided to move back to my apartment to see what condition it was in and to clean it a little bit. It is located in the Kyiv region, very close to the occupied and bombed cities, and most of the nearby territory remained mined.

I remember how I returned to my home. I walked into the entrance, and I had such strange feelings. All the flowers that were on the windowsills were dead. And such an unnatural silence surrounded me.

Also, at first, I woke up every night due to the sounds of demining. After all, demining took place every night. It has dramatically affected my psyche; I can no longer live as before, and I am still depressed.

Although we are all returning a little bit to something similar to life before, it will never be the same again. This war has taken away a lot from us: homes, jobs, relatives, and happiness.

I believe that every Russian who took part in it will be punished in time. And I believe that when we win—and we *will* win—we will be able to live again in a happy and free country.

Leaving a Country Behind

The closer we got to the border, the bigger the crowd became. Women with children and old people; there were also men, some of whom were simply escorting their families to the border. Everyone was tired, scared, and hungry. Some had thermoses of soup or hot tea, while others had sandwiches or snacks. Several children were already so exhausted that their parents had to carry them in their arms. You could hear the children crying now and then, but the adults also had tears in their eyes.

Olena

February 24 was supposed to be another routine day at work. I remember getting ready quietly, without rushing; as usual, I started by carefully checking the schedule on my phone for the coming hours. I work, or rather, I worked in the cabin crew for Wizz Air Airlines. That day, I had a 5:40 a.m. flight to Bergamo.

My base was at Zhuliany Airport in Kyiv, which I reached by cab every day. Ready for my next adventure, I arrived at the airport around 5:00 a.m., which gave me a little extra time to get ready at the office. I remember well that the first person from my crew I saw in the office was Lilla, a new colleague at our base who joined us in early January. Within 15 minutes, our entire crew was ready to start the pre-flight briefing. Unfortunately, we were prepared but did not fly that day.

At one point, I received a call from my mother that the Russians had attacked us. Everyone was afraid of any movement on our eastern side; none of us believed that they would attack us. My first thoughts were related to running away, what to do, and what steps I should take in this situation. We had already forgotten to do any work. In fact, all flights were canceled, and the airport staff told us to go to our homes or shelters.

There was tremendous chaos everywhere. Leaving the airport, I first heard the sound of rockets hitting somewhere in the distance, a terrifying sound that still gives me chills at the mere mention. Ordering a cab was already impossible, so I was forced to make the 25-minute walk home in stilettos. It was the longest and most frightening walk I have ever taken. Now and then, I would check my phone for any news related to the attack or information on what people should do now.

My situation, however, was obvious. I packed all the essentials into my suitcase—documents, toiletries, cash, snacks, and warm clothes. I didn't need many of them, and they could fit in two bags. I closed the windows, turned off the lights, and closed the door behind me. I didn't know if or when I would be able to return. A trip awaited me again, no longer to Bergamo but to Poland. A journey that I was damn scared of.

Amid this terror, I didn't have to worry about shelter; my boyfriend lived in Poland. However, walking out of my building, I saw fear and despondency on people's faces. No one knew what awaited them or what would happen to their loved ones. The city was rife with traffic jams, chaos, and haste, and car horns and engines could be heard everywhere. Never before had leaving Kyiv been so terribly difficult. The lines at gas stations were long enough for several hours of standing. I was grateful that I always had my car at least half-fueled since I never knew when I'd be needed as a replacement at work. It may have even saved my life that day.

Leaving the city took about 3-4 hours, a long time for a city of nearly 3 million people. Now and then, I reminded myself of important things I forgot to pack. Stress and nerves did their job while I was packing, so I tried not to torture myself with this. It wasn't the most important thing. I just needed to get out of the city and head west, as close to the Polish border as possible.

I drove on. It was cold and cloudy, and the temperature did not exceed 10 degrees Celsius. It could have been worse because winters in Ukraine can be very harsh. Now and then, hordes of soldiers passed me carrying heavy equipment. Watching them, I got the impression that they were prepared for a turn of events. Prepared for war. I will never forget the sight.

My family remained in our hometown, the Kropivtse region, about 4 hours south of Kyiv. Their traditional mentality led them to stay in their homes and wait for the situation to develop. They didn't want to flee, to go anywhere. I knew very well that I would not change the mind of my grandmother or mother, who told me to stop wailing and leave the country for Emil.

The trip to Lviv looked very similar, although my memory of it is very blurred. Traffic jams, slow cars, and buses followed each other. Transportation of military equipment made it difficult to move faster, and I usually drove at a maximum of 60 km/h. After another 12 hours, I reached the Polish border in Medyka, a journey that would have taken about 8 hours during normal times. The closer I got to the border, the more complex the situation became. I expected long queues, but what I saw was shocking. So many people were heading toward Poland. I never wanted to believe that this nightmare could finally happen and that so many of us Ukrainians would leave our homes and homeland. Nobody knew anything about what awaited us at the border. Would they let us through? What documents would we need, and will we find any help? So many grim stories were circulating among the people about the attack by the Russkies; now, I find it difficult to recall even one of them accurately. There was so much going on at the time; so many different emotions and thoughts. I was terrified.

I stood in a massive traffic jam waiting for my turn to finally cross the border. The closer we got to the checkpoint, the more and more information people received about the procedures for crossing the border. Among other things, I learned that entering with my car was impossible. Immediately, my thoughts sped up. After all, my two suitcases and this car were now my only possessions. I had heard that some people managed to drive their cars, but I didn't understand why others didn't.

Ultimately, I had to leave my car in a large parking lot near the border crossing. I was calm about my stay in Poland. After all, my boyfriend was waiting for me on the other side. However, I began to get very stressed about what would happen to my car. I know, you might say, it's silly thinking under such circumstances. Rockets are falling on my country, and I'm worried about my car. But when under so much mental pressure, a person sometimes behaves irrationally.

So I locked the car and continued on foot with my two bags, walking towards the border crossing. The closer we got to the border, the bigger the crowd became. Women with children and old people; there were also men, some of whom were simply escorting their families to the border. Everyone was tired, scared, and hungry. Some had thermoses of soup or hot tea, while others had sandwiches or snacks. Several children were already so exhausted that their parents had to carry them in their arms. You could hear the children crying now and then, but the adults also had tears in their eyes. The closer we got to passport control, the greater the uncertainty. No one knew what awaited them next and whether they would find shelter and return home. Wives were unsure if they would see their husbands again, as no man was allowed to leave Ukrainian territory. They didn't know if they were parting with their family for a few days, months, or forever.

As I waited in line with these people, I finally began to think about my entire morning and plans for the day. After all, I had been getting ready for work that same day. I expected a cruise to Bergamo, then some shopping and lunch with a friend. Just another ordinary day and I ended up fleeing my country? With each thought, I could feel the tears starting to come to my eyes. *Will I ever come back here again? And will I ever see my family again?*

After a long wait, I finally arrived at Poland's border control. I saw many border guards, volunteers, and ordinary people who had come to help. Already on the other side of the border, they handed out warm drinks, blankets, and small toys to children. Buses and private cars were waiting for the refugees, ready to go. I realized how lucky I was that I didn't need this help. I thanked God that I was lucky. After all, Russian rockets killed many people at the start of the invasion. Many of my compatriots didn't have the opportunity to flee Ukraine so quickly. Some didn't have a car or couldn't drive it after the fuel at the gas stations ran out. Others were stuck in bus stations wracked by chaos. I was just fortunate.

I've been living in Poland for a few months now and am trying to put my life back together. The war is still going on, and rockets still fall on my country today. It's easy to watch the war from a distant, safe place, but my heart breaks every moment as I watch the Ukrainians who are left behind suffer. Lots of people are still dying there. Despite the immense pain, I follow the news and the events surrounding the war every day. I can see the massive stir in the world from these events. Poland and other countries are helping us as much as they can, and every person in Ukraine will forever be grateful to them.

I'm trying to live normally in Poland during these bleak times. I'm no longer a flight attendant, although I liked that job very much. I now work in the beauty industry as a permanent makeup specialist, a career I want to develop further. My boyfriend and I are planning to open our own salon, but we still need more time and money.

My entire family still lives in Kropiwnicki. Fortunately, the war has not reached there, but there are rocket alerts daily. My mother told me that just one day, two rockets fell on the airport in our city, part of a military school. My apartment in Kyiv is still standing. Fortunately, no missiles are falling on the capital. My family was taken care of by my good friend Masha, who stayed in the capital for the entire Kyiv offensive and checked my apartment when it was safe.

Many people ask me what I think about the Russians. And in my answer, I am always completely honest—I hate the nation with all my heart. It is not true that it is only Putin's war with Ukraine. It is also a war of the entire Russian nation against the Ukrainians. All their words and attitudes towards the war only confirm the thesis that they support the entire offensive against my country. It is simply sick. I don't want anyone in my life to associate us Ukrainians with these despicable terrorists. Let them live in their soap bubble under Putin's regime! I have no friends there and will not have any.

I never believed that my country would be attacked. But now, living in Poland, I'm learning more and more about Europe and the democratic world. I see how Europe can mobilize during challenging moments and send support where it is required.

So I am convinced that from the military angle, Ukraine will prevail with the help of Western countries. I hope I will not have to wait another few years for this victory...

We Did Not Fall in Ninety-six Hours

To be honest, I was one of those people who thought the Russians were our brothers. Since my childhood, people from Ukraine, Russia, and Belarus had been friends. They would visit our countries for work or non-work-related reasons, make families, and live peaceful lives.

Artem

Hello, I am a Ukrainian student, and I want to tell you about the war in Ukraine and what it did to my country. I am thankful for such an opportunity and want to spread the word about the ordinary citizens of Ukraine as well as my friends who are currently serving in the Ukrainian Armed Forces.

War before the Full-Scale Invasion

When the war started back in 2014, I was a school student and did not know much about politics or the situations in the Donetsk and Luhansk regions. I have never been there or had friends from there because I lived in the opposite part of Ukraine. The first two or three years of the 2014 war were the hardest. I remember there was a lot of news about our soldiers who needed help.

Many reports recalled the battles of Ilovaisk, Debaltseve, Donetsk airport, and others. People were volunteering and providing guys with clothes, battle equipment, sleeping bags, food, and other stuff you will need at war.

We also had a new stadium, Donbas Arena, that was built for the Euro 2012 championship. We were proud to have constructed something like that. The stadium ranked in the top twenty-three of the best stadiums in the world. Such a modern place helped us successfully hold the event. Unfortunately, it was shelled and partly destroyed in 2014.

Soldiers had to buy equipment because the government could not fund that. Such occurrences were common during all eight years of war. But even after the full-scale invasion, many people continue to buy everything, paying out of their pocket.

Time passed by quickly. More and more people kept forgetting about the war. It became more or less like a local conflict. Even in the neighboring regions, many citizens did not care. If somebody wanted to fight there, they would be considered a stupid idiot rather than a hero.

That was happening because life in Ukraine became quiet again. The war took on a trench-warfare style. No one was advancing, so many people in the country relaxed. It was not their concern.

When my ex-coworker was going to quit his job, our manager sarcastically told him to go to war. "It is a great option in case you do not want to use your brain anymore," he said. The morning when Russia launched rockets on our territory, the manager fled the country, leaving his team behind with no salary.

Not everyone was like that. Despite the Donbas conflict becoming more and more unpopular, some guys still wanted to help. After all, our soldiers did their best to make a peaceful life in other Ukrainian regions.

Military Exercises and Prewar Days

In all honesty, very few people in Ukraine believed that Russia was going to invade us. Despite our national and foreign media discussing the "military training" of Russia, everyone in Ukraine thought it was a bluff. Nevertheless, the tension was rising.

Many people left the country, others were nervous, and some were preparing shelters, but nobody actually believed in the invasion.

"Russia had similar exercises in the past. Nothing is going to happen. They just want to scare us and the West," I thought. But air companies were canceling flights and IT companies withdrew programmers from foreign countries. The atmosphere in the country was different.

In the beginning, the media was saying that the invasion was going to happen on February 16. My family and I packed our go-bags in case of needing a rushed escape and continued doing our routine. The first things we packed were our documents, some clothes, meds, and money. Then we decided to take some food, water, a thermos bottle, some toothpaste, and matches. I also packed my knife, flashlight, and power bank. I knew that was not the whole list of stuff we needed, but that was better than nothing. On February 16, nothing happened. But the forces were still near the border.

Putin's Speech

On February 21, Putin made an announcement that Russia recognizes the separatist regions. Everyone was following the constant news about fights between friendly and enemy artillery that day, and a lot of people would not sleep. I remember reading many chats on Telegram, where Ukrainians discussed the upcoming war.

The next day, a large number of Russian troops entered Donbas. Everyone was shocked, but many still hoped for the best.

On February 23, Ukraine declared a state of emergency. That night, all the streets in my town were almost empty. Usually, there would be kilometers of traffic jams at that time. Now, cars would occasionally pass by my house. Police were patrolling all over the city. It was very quiet.

To be honest, I was one of those people who thought the Russians were our brothers. Since my childhood, people from Ukraine, Russia, and Belarus had been friends. They would visit our countries for work or non-work-related reasons, make families, and live peaceful lives.

I came to Kharkiv for the first time in 2022, a month before the invasion. It is a big city not far from the Ukrainian–Russian border. I remember a line of Ukrainian and Russian taxi drivers near the railway station who would make, as they said, a quick trip to Belgorod in Russia. I believe the same situation was in Belgorod. It was a peaceful life.

Despite the news, I did not believe they would invade. A lot of people had families both in Russia and Ukraine. There was no reason to attack the foreign country. Unfortunately, on February 24, the Russian Federation launched rockets into Ukrainian territory. Russian forces pushed forward.

I was angry with all the Russians for the first few months. Despite the small protests, I knew they would not stop the war. Putin would rather kill his own people than stop the invasion.

As for now, I do not care much about ordinary Russians, but I hate those who support this war. Still, I would not want to have any contact with any of them. They are betrayers.

The Morning the Invasion Began

The day before the invasion, I went to my grandma's house. She recently lost her sister, and due to the state of emergency, I just wanted to make sure she was ok.

The funny thing about that night was that very few people were actually sleeping. You could see turned-on lights in the windows of neighboring houses. I was surfing the web until 1:00 a.m. when I finally fell asleep.

Between 4:00 and 5:00 a.m., my grandmother woke me up, saying that the war had started. I could not understand what was going on. The whole country was shocked. I immediately grabbed my phone and started reading the news. Multiple air strikes were detected in all the big cities of Ukraine. After that, I heard an air raid alarm go off.

My windows and balcony faced the backside of our yard. It was usually a quiet place. There was a narrow road going up and some little houses on each side of that road. The air raid alarm was not that loud since it was not prepared properly, but you could still hear it in some areas of the town. It was frightening.

I went to the balcony to see what had happened at our airport. I saw the news about it being hit. The place was located one to one and a half kilometers from where I was. There was a black cloud of smoke coming out of what appeared to be an airport. I did not hear an explosion, but one of my friends lived next to the airfield. He said that the explosion was so deafening that he thought that his house was being bombed. Everything in his house was shaking, and it felt like an earthquake.

That place would be bombed a couple of more times later.

My grandmother was a bit shocked at first. After a few minutes, she calmed down, went to the kitchen, and started preparing some food. She talked about her late sister.

"She was born before WWII, could not walk properly, and lived in the village not far from the Ukrainian-Belarussian border her whole life. Maybe God took her so she would not suffer anymore," my granny said.

I knew that things were going to be different from now on. I decided to go home and pack all my clothes. I called my mom, who was a doctor. Despite the war, she was on her way to the hospital. She said it was her duty and that she would continue to work no matter what. My job was to take our clothes, prepare a lot of water in case the city ran out, and buy some canned food. I also needed to take our cats and move them to Granny's.

When I left the house the sound of the air raid alarm could be heard everywhere. There was a traffic jam. Cars were on their way to the Ukrainian border. I saw many people with their go-bags rushing to their relatives. The ones who had already met each other were loading their cars and leaving.

At that time, nobody knew what would happen. We did not know if our army could stop Russia. We did not know if Russia would take all of Ukraine or just stop somewhere in the middle. Many of us were preparing to fight. I remember our enlistment offices were full for the next few weeks.

A friend of a friend was in Kharkiv back then. He was studying in the military academy. Russians had shelled it and killed many cadets that night. The guy said he got lucky because they did not attack the barracks he was sleeping in but the one next to it. It really shocked me because those men were just about my age. Simple guys who just wanted to serve their country.

Our nation became united. There were no more quarrels among the people. Everyone was donating money, volunteering, and providing our soldiers with the required equipment. That was the moment when I felt pride for my country. I was and still am proud to be a Ukrainian.

The Following Days of the War

I was checking the news constantly. The US predicted that Kyiv would fall in ninety-six hours. We did not, but the constant fear and dread were with me for the next few months. But I was not worrying as much for myself as for my family. When the first videos and pictures of destroyed Russian vehicles and captured forces appeared, it was almost a relief. But it felt like it was not over yet.

Constant air raid alarms were terrifying, especially during nighttime. People would leave their homes and head down to the basements of their buildings. In general, we had four or five shelters in the area, so people would just spread out among them. I remember the first night. There were around forty people there.

At first, there was nothing in there. Later we decided to bring some chairs and tables. You could enter the basement anytime, so people would occasionally bring more chairs or simply clean it. But there was nothing much you could do about it. It was a cold and humid basement of a nine-story building where people would drop all the useless furniture made in the USSR. Not to mention that it was locked for most of my life.

Anyways, I told myself that times would be different from now on. I did not know how many hours of sleep I would get. I did not know if the missile was going to hit somewhere near my house or not. I was not sure about anything. I prayed to God multiple times a day, asking him to protect my family. That was my only wish.

My Friends on the Frontlines

After the invasion began, I was full of anger. I could not believe the Russians would do that. I hoped that many of them would disobey the order. Unfortunately, that did not happen. They continued shelling our country.

Some time passed, and we stopped going to the basement. But we still were afraid. I put old coats I found in my granny's closet on the corridor floor. We would stay there for many hours waiting for the air raid to stop.

I had two friends who were in the army. The first one was conscription. During one of those air raid alarms, I decided to contact him. He said he was doing well, and nobody was sending him anywhere. He was just waiting in the military base for things to end. In a few weeks, I could not reach him. His sister told me that Russians had occupied the territory with that base. They could not contact him afterward.

He is still in captivity

The second friend had some military experience. I did not talk to him very often. He went to war in the first two days and was fighting near Izium. He got used to the adrenaline, and anything he said about shelling and warzone came with laughter. One situation he told me about I will remember for a long time because it was not some random story from the Internet, but *his* story.

He told me about two men who went to the nearby village to ask for some food and whatnot. They did that frequently, but this time was different. When they entered the village, they noticed Russians passing by a column, so the guys went to the nearest house and hid in the basement for a couple of hours.

Two Russians had been talking to the owner of the house for a long time. Suddenly, the Russians decided to go to the basement to get some homemade canned food. The moment they stepped into the basement, two guys from my friend's regiment shot all thirty rounds from each rifle. The guys ran away after that.

As it appeared, the Russians were not in the village anymore. My friend did not know what happened to them. They had probably stayed somewhere near it but remained hidden just long enough for the two Ukrainian soldiers to safely go back to their positions.

How We Live Now

Now, after more than six months of war, we try to live normal lives. Restaurants and supermarkets are working. People go outside, meet each other in bars, volunteer, and work. It feels safer to be outside now than it was at the beginning of the invasion. We have enough food and water, and there is no deficit in many cities. Unfortunately, many people from the war zone still experience trouble with food and water.

Air raid alarms are not that terrifying anymore. We just try to stay home during those times. The panic has gone. However, we do not forget our soldiers on the frontlines. People continue volunteering and donating money for equipment, cars, and weapons. Some who are close to the frontlines make food and keep the soldiers fed.

A lot is waiting for us ahead. I hope that after this war, Ukrainians will remain as united as we were at the beginning of it. The war changed many people. We start noticing the small things in life. We miss the peace. But now we know the most important thing about our lives: Freedom is not free.

This Is Not A Movie

One day, she went with my brother to buy some food at a grocery store. They had to wait around four hours to get inside the store. Shooting started on their way back home. They fell on the ground, and my mom said she had only one thought in her head; "Amazing, I'm gonna die because of food."

Marina Petrovska

When I went to school my history teacher always said: "Follow the news but don't take them as it is. Watch it carefully and read between the lines. They always say what's gonna happen. We just don't want to accept it." It's been 10 years since I graduated high school but I still remember these words. This is why I understood what was being prepared for the Ukrainians.

I was always attentive to what was shown on the news but, a few months before the war, I felt something terrible was coming. I caught myself thinking that all the Covid-19 restrictions were nothing compared to what might happen. I remember that I was making a coffee for myself that morning in my small but cozy apartment in Chernihiv when, for a second, I imagined tanks running down the streets. This image was so real that I dropped my coffee cup.

The next day I met up with my friend and told her that I thought war was real this time and would happen soon. We hadn't been afraid the previous spring when Russian troops came close to our border. But this time, it was different. They were ready to invade us, and I could smell that. Before the real attack from Russia, I was already attacked by my thoughts.

I was sitting in a café while my friend was telling me something, but I didn't hear a word. I was deep in my thoughts. And then I heard her say, "How will it be?" I was like, "What?" "The war," she said. At that moment, I didn't know what to say. I couldn't even imagine. All I knew was that I have always trusted my gut, and my gut was screaming: BEWARE.

I raised my concerns to my parents and friends, and no one took them seriously. I was so upset that I wondered if I had just become a victim of the news and was going crazy. When you feel like something bad is going to happen and no one takes it seriously, you start to think it is just anxiety for no reason. I calmed down a bit, and my 'war' thoughts disappeared. I took the attitude, "If it's meant to happen, it will happen." A few weeks later, I received an offer to go abroad and start working there, and I thought this was a great chance to get new experiences to grow as a person and professional. I couldn't even imagine that two weeks after I left Ukraine, I would find myself going through survivor's guilt for not being there for my loved ones when the war began.

I will never forget that day. When I woke up that morning, February 24, in another country, all alone, I checked my phone and got scared. There were dozens of messages from my friends: 'It started.' 'The war has begun.' 'I'm so happy you are safe and not here.'

I thought it was a dream. I remember how my hands were shaking. I couldn't even find my mom's number to call her. My head was such a mess. I couldn't think. I had hundreds of thoughts and, while trying to realize what was happening, I dialed my mother with trembling fingers.

She picked up the phone. The first thing I asked was, "Is it true?" She replied, "Yes. We have no time to talk. We packed everything we could, grabbed our dog and cat, and are heading to your grandmother's place. It will be safer there. I will call back. We are on our way."

My heart was about to jump out of my chest. I began to scroll through the news and couldn't believe my eyes. Everything was even worse than I could ever have imagined. I felt incredibly guilty that I was so far away. I felt guilty that I didn't listen to my gut and gave up on trying to convince my parents that the war would start soon. I felt like I betrayed them.

Day after day things got even worse and, around two weeks later, my town was almost entirely without a cellular network. I couldn't reach out to my parents for a few days, and I didn't know what to do. I couldn't sleep, I couldn't eat, and I was trying to call one hundred times daily, but there was no answer. I was trying to find a way to check on them, so I asked one of my friends who was volunteering to visit them. Luckily he agreed even though it was super dangerous.

People were terrified to come out on the streets because the Russians occupied our town from all sides. The more I watched the news, the more miserable I felt. Finally, a few days later, my friend reached out to me and said my family was fine, but nearly the entire town didn't have electricity, and it was difficult to find a signal in some places. My family was safe. They just couldn't call me.

It was such a relief. A bit later, when my mom finally reached out to me, I told her that I would find a way to get them out of there, at least to make it to the west of Ukraine. But, unfortunately, my parents couldn't do it themselves because my father's car was not working and they couldn't find petrol even if it was. There was a petrol shortage everywhere. People tried to find ways to exchange it with each other in return for large sums of money, in order to take away children and women because it was not clear what would happen next and how bad things would go.

All my parents' friends had already managed to leave the town, and things were getting worse every day. It was really dangerous to go and get food in stores because there were street fights in some districts of the town. Plus, you had to wait hours in line to buy food. My mom didn't tell me much about what was happening, but I monitored the news.

A few days ago, she told me one story that shocked me. One day, she went with my brother to buy some food at a grocery store. They had to wait around four hours to get inside the store. Shooting started on their way back home. They fell on the ground, and my mom said she had only one thought in her head; "Amazing, I'm gonna die because of food." They had to lay on the ground for a few minutes and she said these minutes felt like hours. Then, when it seemed that the firefight had subsided a little, they crawled slowly away to hide somewhere and wait until the fight was over.

But what happened next was even more terrible. Not far from where they were lying on the ground, a rocket fell and stunned them for a while. Mom says that she saw where it fell and fragments dropped near them. The shock wave was extreme. They were literally covered with earth. They lay like that for some time trying to come to their senses and, when they felt that they could finally move, they began slowly heading toward the house. I don't know how many stories she hasn't told, but what she said was the most horrible thing I have ever heard. When you see something like this in the movies it doesn't really impress you. But you get numb when it happens to your loved ones in real life.

I couldn't imagine how my friends and parents felt as they went through all of this, but there was one thing I knew for sure: the countdown was not for days but for hours. So first, I had to get them out of town. I knew that I had to do something because I was in a safe place and still had a chance to earn money. The best thing I could do was start donating and searching for a way to transfer my family.

While I was focused on these tasks, one of my friends called me and said she had managed to flee. She also said that if my parents are ready to take risks, there's one way out. She told me how she ran away step by step. I think at least a few gray hairs appeared on my head as I listened.

The Russians cornered all entrances and exits to the city and didn't want to let people go. There was no green corridor meaning, if you decided to get out of the town, there was no guarantee you would stay alive. They shot columns of cars that were trying to leave the city. She said, "There's a 50/50 chance to stay alive." But she risked it because a 50/50 chance seemed safer than staying there and waiting for a rocket to hit her house. The next thing she told me was hard to imagine even in the worst dream.

She doesn't drive so she had to find someone who would agree to drive her. One person decided to help but, at the last moment, everything changed and the woman said, "Sorry, we can't take you with us." My friend felt devastated, but a few minutes later, she received a call. "Be there (the man named a location) in 10 minutes. Don't be late, or we'll leave." It turned out that woman had found someone to pick up my friend. She rushed as much as possible to be there on time.

When she arrived, she saw there were only women with little kids in the car. As soon as she arrived, they left.

Usually, it takes a maximum of two hours to get from Chernihiv to Kyiv. This time, the road took ten hours, and that was for a few reasons. The first reason was that so many cars created horrible traffic. The second reason was that they had to stop at every checkpoint, which was almost every kilometer. She told me that she saw so many broken and crushed cars on the road, and the dead bodies of people shot by the Russians. At some point, the car she was in also broke down in the middle of the road, and they had to ask other people to pick them up. Of course, it wasn't easy, but somehow she found the next car. A few hours later, this car broke down too and they stopped near the fields. Then, a rocket hit not far from the place where they stopped. All people dropped to the ground. She said it was super scary. She thought it was the end. All dirty and covered in mud, feeling cold and miserable, she found the next car to continue the trip. She said it was the most challenging thing she had to overcome in her life, which is why she warned me that this may happen to my parents.

A few days later, I found a car for my parents and arranged everything. Of course, I was terrified, and I warned them that it was a risk to leave the town. But staying there was also a risk. They had a 50% chance of getting hit by a rocket, being shot by the Russians, or leaving the town, and there was no guarantee they would make it out successfully. I knew I had given a challenging offer to my parents, but I was also ready to accept that they would refuse to go.

They refused to leave and, at first, I was so angry with them because the attacks didn't stop. Eventually, I accepted their decision and thanked God they were safe. Today, things are much better in my town. Many people have returned, the roads are cleaned, and the houses repaired. But the war is not over. From time to time my parents hear the rockets and bombs and explosions. My mom jokes, saying that she already understands the sounds and knows whether it is a rocket or a fighter jet, or if the Ukrainian side is clearing mines or something else. I think my family is used to hearing air raid alerts and explosions.

I know that many people will say I am lucky because I didn't experience everything myself. But I lived through every moment with my family, and I am still worried about them. I accepted that they didn't want to leave the country and that I had no right to ask them to change their mind. We can be only responsible for our own decisions. Now, I hope that the war will end soon and I will finally see my family again.

Coming Home for the Fight

Many women have told us of the brutal rapes committed by Russian soldiers. I also listened to stories of mothers whose daughters were sexually abused for days. A lot of families have lost their children, who were put to death on the streets of cities in mass executions.

We reached Alexiey through contacts in Poland. He used to live and work there, just across Ukraine's western border; when the war started he returned to his homeland to put on a military uniform. Our conversation with Alexiey was repeatedly interrupted due to his active participation in military activities. We communicated using an online instant messenger, and due to the intensity of the fighting on Ukraine's eastern border in the summer of 2022, we experienced several extended interruptions.

Thank you very much in advance for agreeing to speak with us. To begin with, could you tell us something about yourself?

would basically describe myself as a young man who is still looking for his place on earth. I'm only 25 years old, so Ieveryone around me keeps telling me what great prospects I have for life. However, I have come to realize that despite my young age, I already have a few failures on my record, such as picking the wrong college.

You have already spent more than 3 months at the front, fighting for the liberation of your homeland. How did you find yourself on the front lines?

The offensive of the Russian army was a surprise to us, as we did not expect such a rash decision on their part. In my case, active participation in the war effort and service in the army were expected, since I am a graduate of officer school. I did a kind of professional service, which is required after graduating from the academy, and then my friends and I made the decision to go to Poland. We wanted to make some money and experience a better life "abroad". After the outbreak of war, I was forced to return to the country and start my military service. This is how I found myself at the front.

What exactly did you do in Poland?

I went to Poland with two friends; we did all kinds of jobs. At first we worked as cab drivers, which at that time (2 years ago) was a common job for Ukrainian men coming to Poland. But after a while, driving a cab started to seem boring to me, so I switched to the catering industry, working in a restaurant as a sushi master. Now my life has changed dramatically and I am fighting for the freedom of my country. I can definitely say that it's been a dizzying change.

What was the beginning of the war like from your perspective?

Obviously as an active-duty soldier I cannot tell you everything, but I can definitely say with a hundred percent confidence that we were prepared for everything; nothing could surprise us. The attack came from 6-7 directions. At the beginning of the fighting, I was in the eastern area of the country, in the vicinity of Severodonetsk, and then part of my unit was moved towards Zaporozhye. Communication and logistical organization took place extremely smoothly, so that the enemy had no opportunity to create chaos or catch us off guard.

And how is your morale? The Russians continue to put enormous pressure on the defenders of Ukraine.

From the very beginning, morale with us was very high. Every soldier was ready to fiercely defend even the smallest piece of our land. Obviously it hasn't been easy for us, but we have wholeheartedly motivated each other to fight.

Do the weapons that have been coming in from the West give you hope for success?

I'm not sure if I should say this, but without them, in some cases, we would not have been able to successfully defend our country. I freely admit that the weapons coming to us from the West have changed the direction of the war and given us a chance to defeat the invaders. Please don't get me wrong—this does not mean that our Ukrainian army was ill-prepared. But we have had some shortages of equipment and hardware. Things have improved in recent years, but we are still not a major military power. I would like to thank everyone for all the help that Ukrainian citizens have been receiving in Europe, both military and humanitarian.

Apparently you owe several wins to Turkish drones. Even in Poland, a collection was organized to buy another one for you*.

I was aware of the fact of how developed technology is, but I didn't expect the drones to be such an effective weapon.

The war with Russia has shown that such Bayraktars can actually turn the tide of battle. I am glad that we have them.

** A fundraiser was organized in Poland for the purchase of a Turkish Bayraktar drone worth about $5 million. Many Polish celebrities took part in it, and the event was widely commented upon in the media. It succeeded in raising the money, but the company that manufactures Bayraktar drones decided to give the machine for free to Ukraine. All the funds raised were donated to foundations supporting people in Ukraine instead.*

There have been a lot of reports coming in about the crimes committed by the Russians. How do Ukrainian soldiers respond to these reports? Do they motivate you more, or do they have a depressing effect on you?

We are focused on defending our homeland, but any time we read something like this on the Internet (yes, we have access on the frontline to the web, though it is often blocked by the Russians) it causes great pain mixed with an even stronger motivation to fight. We have our work cut out for us, and we want the Russians to suffer the consequences of their heinous acts.

Have you directly witnessed any war crimes committed by the Russians? Can you comment on this?

Thank God, I have not been an eyewitness to the consequences of these crimes, which have taken place throughout Ukraine, though I have heard many stories. Many women have told us of the brutal rapes committed by Russian soldiers. I also listened to many stories of mothers whose daughters were sexually abused for days. A lot of families have lost their children, who were put to death on the streets of cities in mass executions. I still remember the story told by a young girl named Anastasia with a wound on her back, who recalled the moment when one of the f*****g Russians wanted to rape her. He was alone, and she fought back. When he realized she was getting away, he stabbed her in the back with a knife. The girl managed to escape to a neighboring village a half an hour's walk from her village. There came a point when I was no longer able to listen to any more stories, because I realized that they actually were having a depressing effect on my psyche, and I couldn't afford that, because then I wouldn't be able to do my duty properly.

In what language do you communicate with the civilian population in Ukraine? Ukrainian or Russian?

This depends on the locality from which a person comes. I grew up in a town near the Crooked Corner, where most of the population, including my family, speaks Russian. Residents of the Lviv area or towns in western Ukraine speak Ukrainian. In our military, we use both Ukrainian and Russian, as everyone speaks both languages fluently.

Have you lost anyone close to you in this war yet?

Unfortunately, I lost my two best childhood friends. One of them fell in the northern area of Ukraine, defending Kiev and all the towns such as Bucha and Irpin. The other was unfortunately killed during a rocket attack in Kharkov, from which escape was very difficult at the very beginning of the conflict. They are already in a better place, because here, unfortunately, people can still put each other through hell.

At this point, contact with Alexie broke off, due to the increase in the intensity of fighting on the Eastern Front. We managed to pick up our conversation again after a break of several days.

Alexiey, I am very happy that we can talk again after such a long period. What has happened during this time with you?

I, too, am very happy, considering how intense the last week has been in my life. As you can probably guess, we have just launched a counteroffensive in many directions. I took part in the counteroffensive in the Kherson area.

How are you doing in these battles? Is the counteroffensive still being conducted by you?

Yes, the hostilities continue and we are not giving up; we are taking back what is ours, little by little. According to media reports, we have had the greatest successes in the eastern areas, although it is difficult for me to verify this information. Much of it may be made up or unsupported by facts. But it is true that recently we have been winning in every encounter with the enemy. For us in the Kherson area, the intensity of the fighting was weaker, due to the fact that most of the Russian troops have been redeployed to eastern Ukraine. Thanks to that, we were able to penetrate deep into the south of the country without having to engage in any fighting.

We hear from the media that the Russian offensive is becoming less and less effective.

We don't need to get too deep into this question. The Russian troops are very poorly prepared militarily and tactically and have very low morale. Can you imagine fighting for a country that assigns its soldiers rations that expired three years ago? Or would you want to take part in a war equipped with only 60 rounds of ammunition and 2 grenades? We've heard many astonishing stories from the Yonns. The morale of Russian soldiers is very poor and they are additionally being influenced by unrealistic Russian propaganda. It is not difficult to talk about the huge advantage we've gained through the weapons that came to us from the West. It sometimes allows us to gain an advantage and even annihilate all the resources of the enemy in a given area.

And is it true that the Russians are running out of equipment?

I don't believe this is true. Of course, there are rumors that there are old-type tanks or museum exhibits on the streets. I would like to believe that they are running out of equipment, but the attacks they carry out do not confirm this. It should be borne in mind that this is a huge country. Russia is one of the world's military powers (or at least that was claimed until the war with us). For this reason, they are unlikely to run out of equipment. Looking at their equipment sometimes, one gets the impression that it may have been used during the Cold War by their grandparents, but that doesn't change the fact that they are still a military power.

What is daily life like on the front in between battles?

Nothing special happens. Some people read some newspapers that we receive from the local population. Some try to contact their families (if there is cell coverage). Most of us are actually eating and resting. The sheer stress of war and combat, as well as quite a bit of activity on the front lines, gives us a boost of adrenaline at first. But at night or when we feel calm, fatigue sets in and we easily fall asleep. We are constantly aware of falling rockets or bombings, so the quality of our sleep leaves much to be desired. Added to this is the fear that we may not wake up the next day.

Do you have support from the civilian population?

Yes, we receive most of our rations from them. Of course we have our own food, but it is the civilian population that provides us with quality food. We are aware that they sometimes run out, but we get the impression that they often prefer to take food from their mouths and give it to us. As I mentioned earlier, they also provide us with newspapers or even let us call our families if they have better coverage. However, in the areas where we are operating currently, the civilian population is almost non-existent or simply not visible, due to very intensive military operations.

I can only try to imagine what the attacked villages of these people look like. The images on social media are horrifying, and Mariupol has become a grim symbol of this war.

As for the state of the towns, villages or areas, it all depends on where they are located. In the Kherson area, the situation is actually quite good. Of course, a lot of houses have damaged windows, roofs or facades, but after minor repairs they will be habitable again. However, I have also seen many destroyed villages that are unlikely to be able to be rebuilt, which have shared the fate of Mariupol.

Where did the attack on Ukraine come from in the first place?

It's hard to say, because to this day we don't know the real reason for this offensive. Of course, we cannot trust Russian propaganda. In my opinion, it was a terrorist attack on the part of the Russians, aimed at conquering additional parts of our homeland. As a result of hostilities in 2014, Lugansk was taken from us, as well as Donetsk. At the time, the involvement of the Russians was hidden, and the conflict was falsely called a popular uprising in these areas. Whereas now, Russian troops are no longer hiding their attack on our country.

What do you think about Putin?

I can only conclude that his time will come. I hope it will happen soon....

Do you think Putin will be killed?

He has to be, I don't see any other solution.

Do you know any Russians personally?

Before the war, I had several Russian acquaintances with whom I kept in touch. Now they are influenced by Russian propaganda, which has completely changed their mentality. Unfortunately, Russian society is in favor of the war. Of course, there are some people who don't trust the Russian propaganda, but in my opinion, the whole country and its people are rotten, and frankly I wish they would cease to exist.

Where do you think this conflict is leading? When will it end?

This is a difficult question, to which I do not have an easy answer. I can only assume that we will definitely not repeat the situation from 2014, when part of our homeland was taken away from us. This is not politically possible.

It's probably hard to think about this during the war, but do you have any plans, dreams now?

Of course, my biggest dream is to end hostilities and win Ukraine. I don't see any other option. Afterwards I would like to return to Poland and be able to continue my peaceful life, creating some new prospects for the future. My dream is to buy a car and find a well-paying job. I'm also considering continuing my military career, as the pay is quite good. I'm used to military service and I'm not sure if it will be easy for me to suddenly abandon it and return to "normal" life. Time will tell how my life will turn out, but this is what came to mind when you asked me about my future plans. Sometimes I think about starting a family, but I know it won't be that easy. I'm pretty tough, like my father, but after all, I can work on myself. I dream of peace and victory for Ukraine, and I hope it will happen soon. This is now the biggest dream of every soldier on the frontline.

Thank you for your time. What can one wish you in these difficult times?

First of all, health and perseverance, because this will allow us to defeat the aggressor. Also wish me a little luck, because it always comes in handy, especially on the battlefield.

I would like to thank Europe for its support. We will fight to the last drop of blood, including for you. Slava Ukraine!

LIFE UNDER RUSSIAN OCCUPATION

Can there be something worse? Yes—occupation by Russians. Because occupation by them is not about controlling the territory, it is about death. For us Ukrainians, the reasons for Russia's attack on Ukraine are quite obvious and clear. Their goal is only one: genocide. The complete extermination of the Ukrainian nation, culture, and history.

Roman Bohdan

What do you know about war? What do you feel when you think about the war? You are happy if nothing happens. We, Ukrainians, were also happy building our lives and developing our country for the last 30 years. We dreamed of great achievements, set ambitious goals, and rejoiced when we achieved our goals. In short—we lived the normal life of a healthy, modern society that was gradually moving towards the biggest dream of all Ukrainians—to join the European Union and become a part of a large and modern democratic community. But on February 24, 2022, everything changed. In an instant, Ukrainians stopped thinking about familiar things and dreaming of new goals. That day, the thoughts of every Ukrainian shifted to only one thing—survival.

On February 24, 2022 I was on a business trip in Odesa. I woke up around 05:00 in the morning, but not from the alarm clock or loud neighbors as sometimes happens in hotels. In that moment, millions of Ukrainians woke up to powerful explosions in different parts of their cities. What happened that fateful morning? Something that could not be imagined in the modern world. A big war had begun... a war of absolute evil personified by the Russian Federation and forced upon a free and democratic society. Kyiv, Odesa, Kharkiv, Zhytomyr, Uman, Vinnytsia, Kherson and dozens of other cities in Ukraine were attacked that morning by

Russian rockets. They struck simultaneously from the territory of Russia, Belarus, the Black Sea, and temporarily occupied Crimea.

But when I woke up, I could not immediately understand what had happened because my mind refused to believe such a thing was possible. I fell back asleep for a moment. In half an hour, when the next series of explosions sounded, I realized it was a declaration of war by Russia against Ukraine and against the entire civilized world. My first thought was about my relatives who live in a small resort town in the south of Ukraine, in the Kherson region. I understood the Russians would attack from all possible directions in addition to missile attacks. That meant they would strike where Ukraine borders Russia and therefore would inevitably come to our town as it practically borders Crimea.

My parents and my brother with his family live in that town, and I was very worried about them. I called them and learned that Russian troops had not only entered and occupied the town, but had also moved much further north of the town. Fortunately, they were all right. They had mobile communication. We agreed they would stay at home and not go anywhere for their safety. Meanwhile, I hurriedly packed up and without breakfast, left all my important business meetings and moved towards Kyiv, as there was no doubt that the Russians would try to storm Odesa. The road to the suburbs of Kyiv, where I live, took about seven hours. All this time I was in touch with my family, calling them every half hour to make sure they were okay. I understood we would not see each other soon, because this war would not last only three days as the Russians thought. I knew Ukrainians would fight to the end, no matter how long it took, and I was ready for it.

So, when I arrived home in the afternoon, I was extremely tired, more mentally than physically. But I could not rest, because there was an assault from all sides where Ukraine borders Russia and Belarus. Ukrainian military and civilians were dying, and 8 km from the administrative border of Kyiv in the city of Gostomel there were fierce battles with Russian airborne forces for the airport. Explosions were constantly heard in that area. So I moved the most necessary stuff along with water and food to the basement of the house in case of new missile attacks. Then I started looking for where I could be useful to help my country and army. I was not liable for military service and I had never served in the army. Therefore, I did not know how to use weapons, so my effectiveness and usefulness on the battlefield was extremely doubtful. But I did what was in my power. I carried humanitarian supplies, worked on the information front, and supported the army with donations, which I still do today.

And what about my relatives in the occupied town? How did they feel and how did they live? What was life like under occupation? These and many other questions continued to worry me. Every day I called them, or they called me. The Russian army occupied Kherson and the entire Kherson region. But our town is in the deep rear of the Russian occupation so the threat of hostilities in that area is reduced. This gave hope for conditional security and minimized the risk of coming under fire or bombing. But relying on absolute safety was a mistake, as there were many other serious threats to health and life.

So what is life like under the Russian occupation? The answer is simple: like being in prison, an open-air prison. It is not so bad, however, because even if you live in prison, you are still alive. So, what is occupation? Occupation is the illegal seizure by military forces or a group of individuals of part, or all, of a country's territory to gain complete control over the occupied territories.

Can there be something worse? Yes—occupation by Russians. Because occupation by them is not about controlling the territory, it is about death. For us Ukrainians, the reasons for Russia's attack on Ukraine are quite obvious and clear. Their goal is only one: genocide. The complete extermination of the Ukrainian nation, culture, and history. Why do they need to do this? Because they are sick. They are terminally sick with dictatorship, imperialism, and chauvinism, multiplied by wild hate for the entire civilized world and an unhealthy envy of those countries of the former USSR that are now moving into the future.

That is why they want to destroy us, because we are different and better, we are developing and moving forward, while they have chosen the path of degradation and can no longer stop this process. Therefore, they seek to destroy entire nations until there are no developed democratic communities next to Russia. Only their miserable "Russian World" will be left. For decades, Russia's leader has been zombifying his citizens with wild propaganda about Nazis and fascists in Ukraine and Europe. It is unbelievable that the whole country, almost 150 million people believe this crap. These people—ordinary Russians from Moscow and Omsk, St. Petersburg and Syktykvar—now support this savage war and demand even more Ukrainian victims. That is why this is not Putin's war. Absolutely every Russian is guilty of this terrible war.

Therefore, under such circumstances, there can be no normal life in the occupation, and we understand this. The methods and ways of influencing the local population in different occupied territories are different and depend on many factors: on the local military leadership, on the composition of the Russian military and their number in a particular settlement, as well as the moods and attitudes of the local civilian population towards Russia and its actions.

Therefore, the first thing my parents did was clean their phones and home computers, because any patriotic attribute, even accidental, can cost lives. Russians in the occupied territories literally impose brotherhood with Russia on the locals and force them to love Russia. Disagreeing people are tortured and killed. In our place, from the very beginning, a torture chamber was arranged in the basement of one of the educational institutions, and it was never empty. Total repression... People with a pro-Ukrainian position, activists, former military, anyone who poses a threat to Russian ideology are abducted and forcibly sent to that basement. Not everyone survives.

However, the citizens of our town were lucky because Putin has strategic goals for this region because of its geographic location. So, life in our town is not only in basements and torture chambers. People are allowed to move around the city and live a "normal life". But this is just an illusion of life. Two months after the occupation, the Russians finally cut off Ukrainian mobile networks in the occupied Kherson region. Communication with relatives since then and now is only through the Internet. The Internet is a great privilege. Not every occupied settlement is so lucky; only those that have a strategic goal.

Soon life under occupation became more and more unbearable. Lack of goods, medicines, fuel, interruptions of the Internet, looting, criminalization of everything and constant fear of repression just for loving Ukraine—all this made life hell.

That is why my brother with his wife and small child decided to leave their occupied hometown. There was only one open road—to Russia. But they decided to take a risk and go further, beyond Russia. And they succeeded. They were incredibly lucky. Because they had a full tank of gasoline and great luck, they were able to reach Crimea. Meanwhile our parents made a conscious decision to stay at home. They own a small agricultural business and decided not to leave everything to chance, because everything left would certainly be "nationalized" by the administration in the course of occupying our town.

Meanwhile, the occupation authorities did everything they could to create the illusion that Russia is here forever. Russian symbols and flags were installed everywhere, celebrating Russian national holidays was introduced, Russian currency was even put into circulation, the exchange rate of which was equated to the Ukrainian hryvnia, thereby devaluing the savings of citizens and tripling the prices of goods that had already been imported from Crimea.

On the contrary, the prices for agricultural products grown by local Ukrainian farmers were artificially low, so farmers, including my father, were forced to sell the new harvest at prices below cost. At the same time, repression began against teachers who did not want to cooperate with the occupiers and work on their terms, so most teachers quit. However, some were willing to work for Russia.

But the occupation would not be an occupation without military equipment. The Russians cynically placed it in the yards of educational institutions and resorts and didn't try to hide it. All citizens in our town know there is military equipment here, and they know where it is located. Meanwhile, Russian television cynically says Ukrainians are happy to be liberated from the fascist Ukrainian government and they are thanking the Russian military.

Yes, the Russian military really liberated Ukrainians—liberated them from a normal and happy life to live in hell. And this hell has been going on now for more than six months.

FROM UKRAINE TO SWITZERLAND

There is a funny phrase all Ukrainians understand: "Two or three weeks, and that's all." This was the statement made by Arestovych, the popular Ukrainian Youtuber, in the first days of the war. Like other visionaries, Arestovych was confident that the war will not last its third week. Looking back now, I find that phrase funny too; however, deep down I wanted to believe it.

Sofina Kateryna

On February 24, 2022, just before dawn, I was jolted awake by my husband's yelling.

"It has begun!" He ran into the bedroom.

I did not bother to ask him anything because I knew exactly what had begun. I only remember how at that moment everything inside seemed to freeze. My nightmare for the last few months finally came to pass.

All these months we have been preparing; we put aside some cash, kept our phones and power banks charged, and kept all the necessary documents in a separate folder. There were stocks of cereals and canned food on the balcony. The idea of going somewhere and where exactly kept coming up in our minds. However, we did not leave because my husband had a job, the children had school, and we were hoping the worst would not happen.

I remember before the war when I dyed my hair and had my nails done in a salon. I told myself that would be the last time, and about a month later, I was cutting those nails at home. I had ordered some products from a cosmetics site and Aliexpress even though I knew I shouldn't have; I just wanted to believe in a reality where there is no war. Today, all the parcels are probably in our Ukrposhta office in Mykolaiv.

Before the war, I worked online as a marketer and copywriter. I had good clients from Russia. I earned very well for my city. My husband worked in a government agency, in a civilian position. He was in charge of communication devices. The children studied at a local school, a five-minute walk from our house. On weekends, we attended children's workshops on fine arts. We had a chinchilla and a parrot. The parrot was my husband's dream; we bought it after he recovered from a serious illness. I had dreamed about the chinchilla and soon became fond of her. I feel guilty because, when we left Mykolaiv for abroad, the parrot stayed with my husband's father and died shortly after. The chinchilla had to be given to another family. I really miss them both now.

Sadly, life as we knew it ended on February 24. It was scary. My husband and I got up, got dressed, and started thinking about what to do. We read on the parents' group chat that all schools had closed, and my husband did not need to go to work either. We charged our phones and started to pack our bags in the basement. Meanwhile, the children woke up. Trying to control our emotions, we told them that the war had started, Russia had attacked us, but they should not worry because we would protect them.

Life moved from the physical world to the phone. We monitored the news almost every minute and corresponded with friends and family. We were confused about what to do. The morning explosions destroyed the airfield, which was located in our area. After that, the explosions stopped for some time. Taking advantage of the silence, my husband and I went to the store and bought some essentials such as water, dry noodles, snickers, canned food, hygiene products, bandages, and cotton. At checkout, we discovered that credit cards no longer work, so we paid in cash and left.

We headed to the ATM to withdraw some more cash only to meet dozens of people in line. Everyone was wearing a mask; people were still afraid to contract the coronavirus. Some were on their phones, while others were chitchatting, drinking, and eating. We heard that a lot of Ukrainians had run abroad that morning. It was a terrible sight.

Getting home, we installed new applications on our phones; Walkie Talkie, an app for communication when the mobile network disappears, and Alarm, a notification app for when we do not hear a siren on the street. We added new information channels to our Telegram app. Later at night, we couldn't sleep. We all went to bed dressed so we could run outside quickly in case of an emergency.

The next day, in the evening, we packed a few things and left for the basement of the 48th school in the country. There, we met about 30 people. The room was very dirty and unfit for use as a bomb shelter. It seemed more like a trap than a rescue; there was no socket, no heating, and it had only one way out. If a shell ever hit, we would all die under the debris if the only exit was blocked. In addition, as we will find out later, the basement is a real hotbed of diseases and fungi. While we were there, we put the children to sleep on desks and covered them with jackets and blankets. We heard several explosions from far away, and my feet became frozen in my shoes. I wanted to go home to a warm bed but I was scared for the children.

The next morning, we returned home. In the evening, we went to the basement again. This time, there were many more people. We read the news about people that died in a nearby village that was shelled. That night was the longest and the most tense night of my life. Somewhere in the middle of the basement, a sick child was sitting in a wheelchair, experiencing some chronic pain and constantly screaming. People stared sternly at him and his parents. His mother bravely held on, trying to put him to sleep, but he wouldn't stop screaming.

After that night, we never returned to the basement; it was too cold and we could no longer bear the screams. We realized that a basement like this does not provide much protection to us, so we decided to hide in the corridor instead. For the next month, we almost lived there. The children got sick; they had coughs and conjunctivitis. The alarm began to sound more and more often. Every day we had to hide for several hours, as the shells were flying closer and closer.

Several times the Russians tried to capture our city. Enemy tanks drove in the center (we learned about this from the news and eyewitnesses in local groups). My husband and I were once at the store when another attempt to capture the city occurred. The queues at the stores were getting longer and longer; there were very few products available. The children needed to be fed so we waited, hoping to grab at least bread and sausage.

Suddenly, we heard the siren. We checked the news and saw that the Russians had entered our area, close to the occupied Kherson region. The store owner became nervous and wanted to close the store, but we managed to buy something and run home. How grateful I am to the world, the universe, and our Armed Forces that our city resisted the invasion. Otherwise, you would not have read this text. Although I am capable of adapting to and surviving in any condition, I understood that my husband and I would be captured and taken to "the basement," and we were never going to yield or disguise our love for Ukraine and hatred for the invaders, no matter how hard they try. It's good that everything happened the way it did.

Despite the war, my husband remained at his job but seldom went there; he was called in every now and then to repair some devices. I, on the other hand, was left without a job; I broke all working relations with people from Russia, and Ukrainian businesses were not in a position to provide work in my field. I tried to look for alternatives but to no avail.

There is a funny phrase all Ukrainians understand: "Two or three weeks, and that's all." This was the statement made by Arestovych, the popular Ukrainian Youtuber, in the first days of the war. Like other visionaries, Arestovych was confident that the war will not last its third week. Looking back now, I find that phrase funny too; however, deep down I wanted to believe it. And that was why we stayed at home for a month with our children despite the heavy shelling.

Three weeks passed, and then four. One morning, around 8:00 a.m., the city was shaken by the Russian rocket hitting the building of the city state administration. A huge hole was formed and many people died. Watching the first footage from the scene, I remember trembling all over. I realized that "two walls" would not protect me and my family, and we had to do something. I would never forgive myself if something happened to my children.

On the same day, my husband and I made a difficult decision; we decided to flee. I sent a questionnaire for evacuation for me, my husband, and my three children. We started packing immediately; we packed my husband's things separately for fear that he might not be allowed to leave. We did not know what to take. Having heard that volunteers provide the necessary items at the border, we took the minimum we could fit into the suitcases.

Later that day, I went out to the vestibule to talk to our neighbors (a family of four), and they decided to go with us. They called the evacuation service and asked for a place in the same bus. Running away together is not so scary after all.

In the morning, with tears in our eyes, we said goodbye to our loved ones and set off just somewhere away from the gunfire without any plan or anyone waiting for us and sheltering us. During the 15-hour bus ride, we kept an eye on the news as the children slept. We passed all the checkpoints, and luckily, there were no summonses. The road was safe, and we reached the Polish border safely.

As we approached the border, the atmosphere became tense; we were worried that we might be sent back. My heart was breaking with anxiety as my hands trembled. Fortunately, everything went well; we were let through! We were so happy that we didn't know whether to scream or cry. Although we were heading to a completely unknown destination, we were happy to be finally safe.

It was March 30, 2022, and we had just arrived in Poland. We had only crumbled cookies and lollipops left from the food we received from volunteers at the border. After a quick breakfast, we went back to the volunteers to find out what to do next. We were shown the bus stop, which went in two directions: to the railway station (for those who need to go further), and to the refugee camp (for those who, like us, have nowhere to go). We went to the refugee camp.

The camp is the premises of a giant store that caters to several hundreds of refugees. It had rooms with cots, a children's playroom, and a dining room. There were toilets and showers on the street. We understood that we had to spend as little time there as possible, so we took the free beds and laid out our tent. My neighbor and I took care of the children, changed their clothes, and fed them. Meanwhile, our husbands went to look for information about what to do next.

We understood that Poland was already overcrowded with Ukrainians and it would be difficult to find housing there, so we considered all options. We decided to choose Switzerland. Why? Because there was a bus to take us there directly from the camp, as the country had recently opened its doors to refugees, and the volunteers in Poland told us that the conditions there are normal. Somehow intuitively we were drawn there, so we registered for the bus.

Two days later, we were on the bus to Switzerland. We crossed Poland, the Czech Republic, and Germany, and after a long road journey of 22 hours, we finally arrived at a remote canton in Fribourg. You know Gjon's Tears, the finalist of the last Eurovision Song Contest, is from there. I mean, I just wanted to believe that everything was not accidental and fate led us to the perfect place.

On April 1st, we arrived in Fribourg. We were settled again in the refugee camp. This time it was a barracks room, a large gym where bunk beds were placed in rows on one side, and on the other, there was a dining space with tables and benches. The shower was on the second floor, and the toilet was on the street. There were cages for animals/pets. Guards stood at the entrance. The volunteers could speak French. Our wake-up and bedtime were on schedule, and we had three hot meals daily. Every day, a doctor comes in to give prescriptions to those who are sick, as most refugees brought rotavirus from the Polish camp.

We lived in the camp for ten days. The first week, we just ate, slept, cleaned up after ourselves, helped the volunteers, and got medical treatment. There was a café nearby, where we go to get Wi-Fi and call our relatives. In the second week, the head of a volunteer organization came to us with an interpreter; he provided us with information on how to proceed and answered our questions. He informed us that soon we would undergo an accelerated procedure for obtaining the status S, and we will be settled in foster families and dormitories. He stated, however, that not everyone will get the status, and not everyone will be able to move somewhere from the camp at once.

My neighbors were the first to be offered shelter in a host family with an elderly woman. We received our status permit and invitation one day later; a family in another canton was waiting to receive us. We were very happy, but at the same time, we understood that living in foster care was not as easy as it seemed. Still, we had no choice.

We traveled to a new family by way of three transfers using the opportunity of free travel. We dreamed that everything would be good; actually, I could not worry too much because, on that very day, I got sick with rotavirus and I was sick during the whole trip. When we got to the meeting place, an elderly couple (a man and a woman) were waiting for us. They smiled at us and introduced themselves. I became anxious; I couldn't wait to sleep in a proper room, on a proper bed, finally.

We drove home in two cars. A woman drove me and my children, and we spoke English on the way. She asked us what city we were from, and why we chose Switzerland. The road was long. Soon we arrived at a neighboring town, and then into the mountains, at an altitude of 1.5 km above sea level. A godforsaken small village where there is almost no transport and only one shop with a small assortment and high prices. To get from there to the city with some civilization, we had to take a bus (which runs several times a day), then a cable car, then a train several stops, and voila, we arrived at our new home.

Our new home was a two-story house with two entrances. The bathrooms, kitchen, shower, and everything was different on each floor. The owners lived on the second floor, and we got the first, a 3-bedroom apartment. We were to live there for 3 months and then move out.

It was the second half of April, and it was the Easter holidays at school. We were engaged in paperwork, trips to the social service, medical examinations, and so on. We had become friends with our hosts; my husband helped them with household chores, and I treat them with borsch and pastries. We tried to distract ourselves from the news from the homeland, which tore our hearts to pieces every time. We tried to learn French, some common words and phrases such as *Bonjour, Merci, S'il vous plait,* and so on.

My parents were happy that we were safe. It gave them the strength to stay under the daily shelling, taking care of my grandmother, and my niece, while my brother and his wife worked in the same city. We learned to live without any foundation under our feet. However, we were worried about the future. How long will our host help us? What do we do next? When will we return to our homeland, and will there be anything to return to?

Two months passed quickly. Our hosts had decided to evict us from the apartment because they wanted to rent it out to tourists. They wanted to get rid of us as soon as possible, but thank heavens, they found another apartment for us.

The day we moved to our new apartment was a tough one. The whole week before that, we had been cleaning every inch of our old apartment with love and gratitude. We were packing our things little by little. However, we were worried because we didn't know the address of our new apartment until the last day. For some reason, it was hidden from us. As it turned out later, this practice is common in Switzerland. We did not even know at what time the car would come for us. So we found ourselves packing some things at the last moment.

Our new apartment, where we currently live and from where I write this story, is not very far from our old place. It is on the other side of the same mountain but much closer to the city—the capital of the canton. We have two floors of an old but tidy house at our temporary disposal. The house once belonged to the parents of the woman who sheltered us. And, as she said, they would be very happy for us to live there for a while. There was everything we needed inside: a washing machine, refrigerator, oven, dishes, etc. We have two rooms for the children and a bedroom for us. We were so lucky! We realized that now we could get a job, and we could lead a more active social life.

After we moved to our new apartment, we met very kind people. One of them, originally from Serbia, gave us French lessons. These lessons were more than lessons for us; we really needed them. The teachers at the local school adequately catered to the children. Forever in our hearts is a man whom we now call our friend. He understood our situation because he was in Switzerland in similar circumstances many years ago. This person has become very close to us, despite the language barrier. Our Swiss neighbors often bring us vegetables and fruits from their gardens. They have helped us many times without asking.

There is a coach who trains our boys to play football three times a week for free. These people are wonderful.

You know, since the beginning of the war, I no longer believe in God, nor the devil, nor in any justice, but I believe in people now, next to what scum they can be. I saw how people can be people. Real, humane, kind, honest, open, and selfless. I am sincerely impressed by their manifestations. I want to hug everyone who helped us and lent a hand on this difficult path. They say that home is not walls but people, and although I have lost my home, I am happy to say out loud that, here in Switzerland, I have found my second home!

LET ME TELL YOU SOMETHING

His name is Maksym. He is 7 years old. He is my nephew. Originally from Kharkiv, now he lives in the Vinnytsia region, his family is hosted by a young couple in their home. He repeatedly tells the story of his birthday and how it was celebrated in the basement of the house. Unfortunately, the horror of war remains in his childhood memory. Asking Maxim what he wants most of all, the answer amazes everyone. The little boy wants peace and wants to return home and attend school.

Kseniya

The war caught everyone unexpectedly and brought a lot of trouble and pain. It came like a bolt out of the blue. Did anyone expect to wake up on February 24 to the sound of explosions or a call from relatives with such news? Of course not. Until the very last moment, I did not want to believe in such a future and packed a suitcase anxiously. Honestly, I still do not believe that it has happened. I wish it was a dream.

This article is about the full-scale invasion, on February 24, 2022, and the future life of all Ukrainians. We know and remember Russia's annexation of the Crimean Peninsula and the war in Donbas. For eight years, thanks to our army which was able to stop the enemy offensive at the beginning, Ukrainians have been sleeping peacefully in their homes. It is a pity that people who were in the territory of Donbas were forced to suffer back then. It is a pity that the state could not ensure their safety and save those lives. According to statistics from various sources, more than 3600 Ukrainian military and more than 3900 civilians became victims of the war in Donbas from 2014-2021, and almost two million people were forced to move. Of course, there are still those who live in the occupied territories and support the actions of the Russian Federation, believing the propaganda. We will not analyze why this happened and who is to blame as that is a topic for a separate article.

So let's talk

How did it all start for me? At three in the morning, I was talking to my boyfriend while he was going to work. He was working abroad, while I was in Vinnytsia, Ukraine, at the university finishing my studies. We were happy and joyful, planning our future together. But around five that morning, life changed completely. My boyfriend was the first to call me, but it was still early and all attempts to receive information from him and various telegram channels were unsuccessful. I still remember how I had tried to calm him down and say that it could not be, it was all fake.

Around eight that morning, I heard a rumble and then an explosion. Unfortunately, I did not fully understand that it was the arrival of missiles... But it was scary. The siren started to sound, it became very noisy around. People were leaving the city. Relatives and friends began to call and message, there were so many questions. So much fear and terrible panic. There were proposals to leave the country, but we stayed. At the first opportunity, I went to my parents in the region, it seemed safer there.

Day after day I was monitoring the news. In the first days of the war, the dean's office and teachers of the university realized that students had no time to study, so we started "holidays". You know that feeling when you always wanted to rest more and then you have such an opportunity and the desire disappears. That's exactly what happened here. Attempts to distract from the war for the first two months were in vain. My family and I had our noses glued to the phone and in the news all the time. It's a terrible feeling and understanding that a missile may come nearby...

As for arrivals, it was relatively safe in every town or village of Ukraine, which is far from the zone of active hostilities. I also thought that it couldn't get to my town, but... on the second day of Easter, I woke up again to the whistling and explosion of two rockets. Then there was an alarm, which I had successfully slept through. When I went outside, I saw a big black column of smoke. Later the local media and the military administration wrote about the missiles hitting the information structure, namely the railway tracks. Fortunately, this hit was on the outskirts of the city and no one was seriously injured. I will remember that morning for the rest of my life.

I hoped never to hear that sound again, but I heard it repeatedly... my family always used to go to my grandmother's house and plant a vegetable garden there. So, it was spring, and we were planting garlic, with a tractor roaring in the neighbor's garden, but my mother and I still heard the whistle of rockets. Six rockets flew over us in a matter of seconds. A few minutes later, the media wrote about arrivals in Ternopil and Lviv... such realities are terrible.

I remember the situation in Vinnytsia. I went to the hospital to take some tests and meet my friend afterward. I heard the siren, hoped that everything would be okay, and hurried to the hospital because I was already late. When I got to the hospital, I recorded a video message to my boyfriend that I was fine, that the city was calm and I hoped for a quick release. Five minutes later, my boyfriend received a video message where I was hysterical, tears and horror in my eyes, and the sounds of firefighters and ambulance sirens were all around. After the missile flew over, I did not have time to count to three, as the explosion had already sounded. The rocket hit a civilian information structure, which I was passing by in the morning, and my friend was passing by about 20 minutes before the explosion... you cannot neglect safety, you must seek shelter.

The war continues. In addition to missile hits, I also remember the successful work of air defense. Just recently, our air defense shot down a missile over the city. The air raid began a few minutes before the explosion and even the sirens did not stop buzzing. Only a "snake" of smoke remained in the sky. There was another case with the shooting down of an aircraft over the region, which my family and I saw. Then the media wrote about the downing of a Russian UAV that appeared from somewhere and flew very, very high.

Throughout the war, my family and I have been supporting the country and the army and we volunteer often.

I often send donations to various available fundraisers for ammunition, medicines, and equipment for our army. No one and nothing but your nation and your dear people motivates you more to overcome the enemy, to destroy his desire to destroy us.

Let's continue

To write this article, I had to talk to many people of different statuses and ages who experienced different situations in the cities of Ukraine. For convenience, each story is written separately and in detail in the format of an interview, so as not to intertwine thoughts, desires, and emotions.

Maksym from Kharkiv, 7 years old

His name is Maksym. He is 7 years old. He is my nephew. Originally from Kharkiv, now he lives in the Vinnytsia region, his family is hosted by a young couple in their home. He repeatedly tells the story of his birthday and how it was celebrated in the basement of the house. Unfortunately, the horror of war remains in his childhood memory. Asking Maxim what he wants most of all, the answer amazes everyone. The little boy wants peace and wants to return home and attend school. Only by communicating with this child, do you begin to understand what a bright sun he is.

As soon as Maksym's family managed to leave the shelled Kharkiv, they came to us and the first few days we all lived together. They lost their apartment; their house was destroyed by a direct shell hit and their job in their native Kharkiv. Maxim needed communication, so I was like his psychologist. Now the boy is fine, he is in good condition, but he is very afraid of the sound of the siren.

The story of Anastasia from the Kyiv region is presented on her behalf at her request, without changes, everything as she wrote:

"I am 12 years old, I dreamed of traveling around the world, dreamed of a home in which there is peace, but one day changed everything. I woke up at 6:00 a.m., I heard some humming. At first, I thought it was my dad and mom going to work, but when I went out to them, I realized what was happening. As it turned out, the war had started. My dad went to the gas station, my mom was packing, and my grandmother said that she would not go with us, that we would go alone (we were going to go to the Vinnytsia region to other grandparents).

My younger sister was sleeping, and the windows were shaking. It was the bombing of Boryspil (we are from the Kyiv region). I started to collect things that I would need in the first place. My dad called and said that there was no gasoline anywhere. When he arrived, he said that we should be at home and then we would decide what to do. I was very scared because it was the first time I saw a real war, the first day of the war we just stayed at home. After all, we had no other choice.

All 4 days of the war my family and I lived like ordinary days, our town was not bombed, so we were a little calm. At 1:00 p.m., my friend from Kyiv wrote to me, they were going to their dacha, which was located in our village. Then my friend wrote that it was colder in their dacha than in the cellar, so she came to spend the night in our house. We supported each other as much as we could. But on the first day, when they started bombing us, my dad went to the Defense Territory without saying anything. My mother was crying, my grandmother too, and my father was holding back tears, but as soon as he started hugging me, he started crying and scratching me. I felt pain, not physical, but moral. I stood in a hug with my dad for 5-10 minutes, then I went to my room to cry. Since then, my dad has been defending our town.

It was Sunday after my friend spent the night at my house, and my dad was in the territorial defense. I woke up not from the explosions, but from the fact that my mother was packing her suitcases. I found out that my father wanted to send me, my mother, and my younger sister to a quiet town nearby for a while, and then to Poland. We were picked up by his colleagues from the territorial defense, we left, and my grandmother stayed :(. When we arrived at the place, we were picked up by a volunteer, as it turned out, it was the mother of my former friend, she took us with love, then I met her son again. Sometime on Sunday we were in their house, in the end, we even heard shots, we were hiding in the corridor.

And so, the day of departure from Ukraine came, and the volunteer's son went with us. The road was incredibly long, we were waiting for our train for 4 hours, then it was delayed for about 7 hours. Then there was horror! Everyone was pushing, and some woman who spoke Russian was spitting, thank God we got on the train, some people couldn't get on and stay. Then everything was fine, I wish everyone well, everything will be fine, Ukraine!"

The story of Zlatoslava from Mariupol captured my heart. In her story, she put her love for her hometown and the phrase: "I stopped being afraid of a shell hitting my head because it's fast." Here is her story:

"24.02.2022 is the date that will never be forgotten. This is the date that changed the lives of millions in an instant, this is the date when blood began to flow on our land. We will never forgive this. I am a student of Mariupol State University, I have lived in Mariupol all my life, admiring my city and its people. Since the aforementioned bloody date, I started to keep my diary. The diary of a Mariupol resident who saw with her own eyes all the horrors of war and genocide of our people.

The first days of the war were quite easy but exciting, my heart broke more from the news of Kharkiv or Kyiv. We knew what the war was like by the example of 2014, everyone was afraid, everyone was scared, but we were sure that even if something started in the area of our city, the shells would not fly into residential buildings. We said: "These are residential buildings, there are PEOPLE here." How much we were mistaken. "In politics, there are no people, but ideas; there are no feelings, but interests. In politics, you don't kill a person, you remove an obstacle, that's all." This is a quote from the book "The Count of Monte Cristo" by Alexandre Dumas. A book that helped me to hide from the darkness outside and put on my "armor" from the excitement of the sounds of falling shells and bombs outside the window.

On the first day of spring, we lost power, which meant the water would soon be cut off. The power outage meant a complete absence of sirens, but we learned about the air raid from the Internet. On March 2, after the mobile communication was cut off, we learned about the air raids only by the sound of falling bombs and the sound of the plane flying above us. The first days without communication were the most difficult because the complete ignorance of what is happening is simply infuriating. Then it was worse because hope for rescue was decreasing every day. After the curfew, we heard gunfire, which meant the elimination of saboteurs, it could not but rejoice.

After the water was cut off, the gas was cut off, which was scary, but we got used to it. We collected technical water from the gutters after rain or collected snow and cooked food on the fire. When there was no possibility to chop wood, we broke chairs. It was a strange feeling on the first day of bonfires in our city, if not for the constant screams: "The plane, hide!" and the whistling of shells, you would think that it was the first of May and everyone went out to the barbecue.

Every day there was less and less food. There was not a single store with food left. Then I rethought the essence of death, or rather its cause. I stopped being afraid of a shell hitting my head because it is quick. But to die of hunger in the siege of the city is another thing. It would be even worse to die for a long time under the rubble or because of injuries. I tried not to think about death, but in such a situation it just pops into your head and you can't get rid of it. Every day you think about whether this is your last day or not.

Sleep is a separate topic of conversation. You cannot sleep normally when you wake up from every rustle and every time it seems that a shell fell somewhere nearby. The worst thing happened to our family on the night of March 11. It was a quiet evening, no matter how strange it may sound. So quiet that it was scary. We were dozing off when at 11:00

p.m. we heard the noise of an airplane, then a crash. We jumped up and ran into the hallway. A few seconds later, an air bomb arrives in the neighboring house, right next to ours, and our windows were smashed together with the frame and fly into the apartment, along with the interior doors. The feeling is like an incredible fear mixed with confusion. You seem to know that you need to run to the basement, but the ringing in your ears and the inability to control your body simply prevent you from reacting adequately to the situation.

Every night we were blown up by the hum of the plane, and the worst part of it was the waiting. When you hear it, you understand that it is flying somewhere nearby, and maybe even above you, and you just wait and count the dropped shells. As we understood (I do not even know if it is true or not), one plane has 4 bombs. So we counted them and prayed.

Sometimes we said, "When the war is over, we will..." and at that moment you think, will it end at all? And if it does, at what price? What will happen to us next? And a million other questions to which there are simply no answers. And in general, it was very unusual to talk about this situation "war", because it took a long time to realize that in the 21st century there is a place for this outrage. And all this just because of one crazy old man and his no less crazy pack of dogs.

I left Mariupol on March 15. It was scary. Very scary. You drive through the city, you see just devastation, you see burnt houses, and dead people, whose neighbors are covered with rags or jackets. You look at it and it becomes difficult to breathe, difficult to think, difficult to react to it somehow. You think about your family, about your friends, about everyone important to you and you understand that you can do nothing about it and do not know how to help."

Mykhailo from Kherson also told his story, which is worth reading:

"On February 24, I was going to work from a small village near the city to Kherson as usual. But in the morning I heard explosions in the distance. While my friends and I were traveling on an intercity train, all excited because we did not know what was happening, we saw flames from the direction of the well-known Chornobaivka: the airport was burning.

When I arrived at work, I realized that something terrible was brewing and tried to contact the military registration and enlistment office, but it did not work. The street was a mess, with accidents at every step, and kilometer-long queues in all shops, pharmacies, and ATMs. I called my beloved (although we were not even together yet) and told her to pack her things. We tried to leave the city for a village located between Kherson and Mykolaiv. I thought it would be safer there, but there were no buses or trains.

It took us five hours to find a way home, but it was all in vain, so we decided to hitchhike. And we succeeded, most people had already left and the city was almost empty. We were helped by men who were going home to Chornobaivka, it was almost half of our journey. Then we went on foot until we met another kind man. We reached the village and waited for what would happen next, thinking that it would be safer in this village (Blahodatne), but I was wrong.

The first column of Russian equipment appeared 4 days from the beginning of the war. They were defeated by our troops, and the three remaining vehicles were burned by the locals with Molotov cocktails. Three Russian soldiers surrendered to the local community and my teacher and I went to the vehicles, trying to get everything that our military might need. We took out first aid kits, military documents, machine guns, and grenades. All this together with the prisoners was handed over to our military in Mykolaiv, and we stayed to wait and patrol our native village.

But the orcs came faster than we imagined, and at that moment a small branch of hell opened next to us. They dug in around the village and arranged their equipment so that no one could get out. We tried to report their location to our soldiers, and many of us, including me, started to receive text messages with threats from the Russian "army".

They turned off our electricity and water and because of the constant shelling, we hid wherever we could. But when we started to run out of drinking water and food, my beloved and I went to our friends who had a generator to get water and charge our phones. On one such day, March 15, everything changed dramatically for the worse. Orcs started firing mortars at village houses. And in the morning when I went to my friends to charge my phone, I was asked to help collect the corpses and bury them. Of course, my teacher and I agreed and, having gathered more men, we went to bury them.

The cemetery is located outside the village near the orcs' position, and we had to dig graves and bury the dead from their shelling under the sight of their f*****g machine guns. Later in the evening, when my beloved and I were walking home from friends, I realized that I wanted to cut out all the Russians, and all because they started firing mortars at us right on the street. And then I saw hell, broken houses, and my beloved screaming in pain.

While my beloved was lying on the ground bleeding, I was lying on top of her, covering her ears and hoping that this horror would end soon. Gathering my strength, I looked around and saw nothing but dust and blood. The shelling continued, the shells that hit us fell 15 meters away from us and destroyed the house. I got up, examined my beloved, and saw her wounds, bones, and blood. I took her gently in my arms (she was conscious) and with cries for help began to carry her as quickly as possible to the nearest house, it was the house of my teacher.

At my cry, a man came out of the house that had just exploded and helped me carry her to the yard. Then there was horror. With the sounds of shelling and her crying, I tried to stop the bleeding on her leg, part of the skin was gone, and there was nothing left of the sneaker, but we provided first aid as best we could. My teacher, my sister, and my father came out of the cellar at our cry.

The shelling continued, and we brought her wounded down to the cellar, where there were children and women. I could hardly hear anything, except for the noise in my ears. We found all her wounds and began to provide medical assistance, she was conscious. The shelling was less frequent, but still going on.

After an hour and a half in the cellar, I felt that I could barely stand on my feet and my eyes began to darken. As it turned out, I was standing in a pool of my blood. The teacher helped me to find my wounds. My legs were bleeding, my buttocks were torn by shrapnel, there was no skin on my pelvis, and my legs and whole body were beaten. The blood did not stop, I began to lose consciousness, but did not stop joking.

Then the Russian orcs came and I started asking them to take her to the hospital, but they gave us bandages and morphine and said they could not do anything else.

My family came and when the shelling stopped, we were taken home and the longest night of my life began... [Mykhailo's story ends here]."

Let's look at the situation from the other side, from the military. Here is what Timur says "On February 24, I probably exhaled a little—at least somehow the situation became clearer. Do you know what they say? Better a horrible end than a horror without end, says Timur Plyushch from the 24th separate mechanized brigade named after King Danylo. At that time, his unit was near Katerynivka in the Luhansk region, near the occupied Pervomaysk. The situation escalated earlier: on February 17, the first massive shelling along the entire contact line began. I talked to the guys and commanders—no one believed in a full-scale invasion. But everyone understood that something was being prepared. On the night of February 22-23, our positions were shelled with "Grad" for the first time, and from 23 to 24—on the contrary: the night was quieter than the previous one. And in the morning, I open the news and see what has started."

At the beginning of the article, I wrote about Donbas. I managed to find a military man from Donbas. He saw the development of the situation from the inside in the east of the country in 2014. "After it became clear that this was not some "misunderstanding", but a real war, I left the uncontrolled territory of Ukraine and signed a contract with the Armed Forces," he says.

"On February 24, I was met at home with my family. Like most Ukrainians, we woke up from the explosions somewhere between 4:00 and 5:00 a.m. I was scared in the sense that I did not understand what was happening. The nature of the explosions was such that I had not heard before. In 2014-2015 it was mostly artillery, no air defense, missile systems, let alone air strikes were used," says Ihor. "In the morning, the family decided to leave Kyiv. First to Vinnytsia, then to Ternopil, and finally settled for several months in the Kopychynets community. It took 3-4 days to get oriented, and then I started looking for ways to help. Because just sitting on the couch is not an option. You can go to the roof, the man recalls. Then I found people in Ternopil whom I knew from the time when I was in the hospital. They organized a volunteer warehouse and began to carry protective equipment for the military from abroad."

The last story of Donetsk resident Mykola begins in 2014. "Until 2014, I lived in Donetsk, and worked as the chief director of the TV channel "Donbas". In 2009, my wife and I had a son. I repaired my house, which is located 3.5 kilometers from Donetsk airport. In 2014, I could not imagine that it could be that it would lead to the occupation. There were no preconditions. I was amazed by the rallies on Lenin Square—they were not attended by Donetsk residents, they were visitors—they took pictures near McDonald's, and did not know their way around the city. Donetsk residents did not believe that something would come out of these few rallies, they treated these people as urban madmen.

On the day of the liberation of Sloviansk, I realized that the point of no return had come in Donetsk—when I read the news that Girkin and the whole gang had entered Donetsk. But I continued to work, despite the "decree" banning the activities of the channel and me in particular. We were stormed several times, and finally, the channel was taken. They put us under machine guns. My wife, who worked in the tax office, did the same. It was unpleasant. But even after that, we stayed in the city, we did not want to run away. We believed that Donetsk would be liberated, because how can it be that they are trying to drive us out of our city. When the fighting for the airport started, we could hear it at home. One day we were playing ball with my child, who was almost five years old at that time, near the house. It started to thunder, and I offered him to go home, and he said, "Let's stay, it's not close." Then I realized that the child's psyche began to adapt to these terrible processes, and we decided to leave.

We went to Mariupol for a few weeks to the sea, as we thought then, to wait it out. Then it was not morally difficult, because we were sure that we would return. When we moved to Dnipro, it became harder, because we realized that we could not go back and we would not return soon.

Later I was transferred to work in Kyiv, but neither the capital nor Dnipro became mentally close to me. In 2018, I was offered the position of head of Mariupol television, and we moved to the city. Only there I felt at home—Mariupol reminded me of Donetsk in some way. My family lived there for the three happiest years of our life. Everything suited us, the sea, the climate, the location of the city. We lived in pleasure. On weekends we went to the sea and communicated with friends. In January 2022, we seriously thought about buying a property.

Reports of a possible invasion were not something wild for Mariupol residents. We understood that there could be an escalation on the part of the Russian Federation, but at the same time, we knew that the city's defense was very clear. At the same time, I expected that it was all political bargaining, that Russia was trying to persuade us to do something, and hoped for diplomacy.

On February 24, I did not even wake up from the explosions. I got up, as usual, checked the news, and learned about the Russian attack on Ukraine. I understood that there may be problems with communications, food supply, and money in ATMs, so I went and withdrew all the cash, and bought food, and water, as I thought at the time in sufficient quantities. I bought candles, lighters, and medicines and was calm that I had protected my home and family. As it turned out, there was no need to withdraw cash, because money was worthless during the blockade.

I thought that in 2014 I saw the war. I took various pieces of training, how to behave under fire, in case of capture, in battle, and thought I was ready for anything. However, the year 2022 showed that I was not ready for anything. It was hell.

At first, the city was left without electricity, water, and heating. When we were blockaded, the supply of food, fuel, and cash stopped. Then mobile communication was lost. People got into an information vacuum. It was scary. At the same time, the process of survival began. The exits from the city were already closed by the Russians. Fuel supplies had also stopped. I had a full tank, but I was saving gasoline because I understood that the car was my evacuation resource. Every time I left the house, my wife and son said goodbye to me as if forever. During the first days of the blockade the shops were still working, they were selling the leftovers until the warehouses were shelled. Only 20-30 people were allowed to enter the shops, all the rest were waiting outside, and it was up to a thousand people, the queues were crazy.

On March 6, an hour before the store opened, my neighbor went there to take a queue near the entrance. In 20 minutes, as the concierge later told me, he knocked on the door, took a couple of steps, and fell. Blood was flowing from under him. My neighbors and I jumped out screaming. As it turned out later, a mine or a shell fell in that area. A neighbor later said that people in the center of the queue were just torn apart. He somehow managed to get home with two fragments in his thigh and under his shoulder blade. He was saved by the fact that a sanitary epidemiologist lived on the first floor of the house and gave him first aid. In addition, it was lucky that the policeman's family had been evacuated to our house the day before and his colleagues came to pick him up that morning. The police were still working then, taking out the wounded, counting the bodies. So the police took the wounded neighbor to the hospital, the same children's hospital which was destroyed by a bomb on March 9. He had been discharged the day before.

When the hospital, which is 800 meters away from us, was attacked, we thought it was a bomb dropped on our house. He jumped up, and the windows of the hospital were bent and covered with earth. This neighbor was crying because he was alive and also because he saw how many children were left there.

One day I went to the office to get water and saw a picture I will never forget: puddles of blood on the road and human brains eaten by a stray dog.

On the morning of March 13, I was shaving in the bathroom, and there was a wild sound. You can't call it an explosion, a crack. It's a sound that awakens primitive fear in you, consumes you. The blast wave pushed me in one direction, then in another. Then this sound was heard twice more. When my son saw his room, it was horror. Not only broken windows but also twisted frames, literally torn from the walls. Extremely heavy oak doors just flew out. The furniture was upside down, everything was in pieces. As it turned out, the plane dropped three missiles that fell 50 meters from our house. After that our house was uninhabitable. We all went down to the basement and slept in the whole house. Children on mattresses, elderly people on chairs. It was the warmest room. Let me explain what was considered warm then, plus 12 degrees in a room where there were many people. Outside, the temperature reached minus 10 degrees, in apartments with broken windows it was minus eight. People put on everything they could.

Every day I went up to the 10th floor, where I could catch the signal, and recorded small video blogs about the situation in the city. On March 14, I did the same and saw information that people were leaving through the "green corridors". I gathered the residents of the house and announced that we would leave tomorrow. I understood that if we stayed, we would have scant chances to survive. The next morning, we set off in a column. As it turned out later, there were 2500 cars in the column. We were driving slowly, there were many craters from explosions, debris, and broken wires. Explosions were heard nearby, shells were falling. I did my best not to let my son look out the windows because there were bodies of people everywhere.

It was completely different from leaving Donetsk in 2014. We rented an apartment in Zaporizhzhia, we have no plans now, we live one day at a time."

There are hundreds of such stories, and millions of them have a common goal—the victory over evil. Over the torture of the Ukrainian nation. The Ukrainian people.

SOUND OF MISSILES

Night alarms usually happen at the same time. It seems that invaders have a schedule. The first one usually happens right after midnight, then they wake us up in the middle of the night at 3:00 a.m. and finally around 5:00 a.m. This is what our usual night looks like. It seems that they let everyone fall asleep and then wake up, time and time again.

Yuliia Tatarchuk

Two sleepless nights had their effect. This night I missed three air alarms. Even though they are so loud that it seems that they are installed directly in my head, that night I heard none of them.

The day before yesterday, several missiles flew directly above my house and then exploded near it. It took some time to recover and stop shuddering from any sound. Yesterday night was stormy. It seems that not only people and animals suffer from the war. Nature is shocked by all this horror that happens around. I don't remember a single summer here in Ukraine that had so many thunderstorms. It feels like nature is trying to wake people up from this nightmare and convince them to stop the crimes. Unfortunately, the boundless power of nature is inefficient in changing people's minds.

Loud thunder and bright lightning that previously didn't bother anybody became a real problem in our new reality. When I used to hear thunder, I thought nothing except that the day would probably be rainy. This summer, thunder made me, as well as everyone around, stop and think: "Thunder or a missile?"

And the worst thing about that is that several times I did make mistakes. I was sure I heard thunder during the night but that was an explosion. That's why stormy nights became very anxious and totally sleepless. It became usual to receive messages from friends and family with the same question: "Thunder or a missile?"

At those moments I felt so much responsibility for the safety of the people I love. They were waiting for my opinion and hoped I would say that it was thunder. As if I could know for sure or if I was an expert in detecting the sounds of weapons. I also used to write to them hoping to receive some calming news, even though I knew they couldn't be sure. It's a big luck that we have news channels on Telegram. They turned out to be very useful. It is such a pleasure to receive a message saying that it was thunder and not an explosion.

After I witnessed the flash of light and saw how the rocket flew near my house, the lightning also made me stand up and look for shelter. Even though I can clearly see when it is raining, I can't be totally sure that it isn't a missile at this specific moment. That's why it is impossible to fully relax during stormy nights. Only exhaustion helps to eventually fall asleep.

There's one more interesting fact I noticed. Night alarms usually happen at the same time. It seems that invaders have a schedule. The first one usually happens right after midnight, then they wake us up in the middle of the night at 3:00 a.m. and finally around 5:00 a.m. This is what our usual night looks like. It seems that they let everyone fall asleep and then wake up, time and time again. Sometimes, there are more alerts and even explosions. One sleepless night isn't a big problem. But when each night during seven long months is the same, it becomes a problem.

Of course, I should admit that I became more used to the danger. When I recall the first alarm, that was not only the first alarm of this war, but also the first real alarm that I had ever heard in my life. To tell the truth, it makes me laugh.

When the war started, I tried to do my best and prepare everything that our authorities advised us. Luckily there is a very good basement under my house. As all my neighbors seemed to be shocked and scared, I felt that it was me who should check it. I went there, looked around, and then moved deeper to check the second exit. It was very important to be sure that we had another exit to be able to escape if necessary. The tunnel was very small, something about 80 centimeters in height. And it was very dark and wet. It wasn't the best adventure of my life. The exit was perfect and that was great.

When I went home, I started collecting all the stuff I thought my family could need in the basement. I put food, water, medicines, spoons and plates, warm clothes, all the tools I had, candles, documents, and much more. Eventually, I got several heavy bags but at that moment they didn't scare me at all. Each day I kept on adding new items and felt that I was doing a great job.

The day when the first air alarm in my city was turned on, I was alone at home. And I heard it. Everything happened so unexpectedly, and I was so scared that I grabbed all my bags and rushed downstairs—six floors down to reach the basement. Along the way, I was knocking on my neighbors' doors in case they missed the alarm. It still seems a mystery to me how I managed to run downstairs with all those bags that weighed much more than half of me. Firstly, we used to run downstairs each time with all those bags both in the daytime and during the night. Then, we did the same with only one bag. Then we all felt so exhausted that we stopped running to the basement during the night. Now we don't go to the basement at all and we left a small bag next to the door.

All these memories make me laugh because they show that I didn't actually understand reality. I thought that I would always be able to run six floors down and then up with heavy bags and continue working with the same effort. I'm not able to. Neither can other people. We managed to get used to the danger. We go shopping, kids are playing in parks, people get married and celebrate birthdays. When the alarm is on, people tend to look at each other as if looking for someone who could tell them that everything will be fine this time.

You never know which target will be the next. I realize that sometimes when I need to go to the supermarket, useless analysis starts in my mind. It seems that my brain is trying to choose the best direction. It looks for some logic. What buildings are there around that supermarket? Could they be the potential targets for the missiles? Maybe another one is better? Which path to choose? Those are completely useless questions as there's no logic in the explosions. Just a chance.

I'm very happy that people try to be optimistic even though I see that it's not so easy and not everyone manages to continue living without sedative remedies. What this war gave personally to me is that I started to notice more.

I remember walking with my friend once. We had to postpone our meeting several times because of explosions that happened right before the meeting was arranged. When we managed to gather, the weather was perfect and we enjoyed the walk. The atmosphere was so peaceful and nice that we sometimes could forget about the war. As usual, at some point, the alarm was turned on. My friend started to worry, and I said that there were good places to hide around here. Her reaction was immediate and very sincere. She said that she hoped we wouldn't have to lie on the earth because she was wearing her favorite dress. We both started laughing. Having the danger of a rocket falling on your head wasn't as scary as the possibility of getting your dress dirty. It was so pleasant to understand that a piece of our previous peaceful life was left in our minds.

Another curious fact that I noticed was that, predictably, the topics of people's talks changed dramatically. Nobody is now surprised when they hear girls or women discussing Himarses or Gepards and their differences from other kinds of weapons or the speed of missiles and the time you have to hide after it's launched. Believe me, old ladies walking in parks know how many tanks and planes we have more precisely than any ministry of defense does! Indeed, we all received new knowledge and new wishes. To tell the truth, if the war doesn't stop by the New Year holidays, I think that most of us will wish to get more weapons.

The value of things changed dramatically during the war. Of course, we all want to live in beautiful houses with modern furniture, wear good clothes and have the newest gadgets. But what's the use of all this stuff if your life and your home are in danger? I experienced being a refugee for three months. I clearly remember packing my stuff in the suitcase. There are so many necessary and valuable things at home, but you can't take them all. You can't even take the biggest part of them. You can afford only one suitcase of your previous life. I remember going by bus, passing signs saying that the territory was mined. I remember a cold night while walking towards the border with heavy bags across the field. Then, there were months full of moving from one place to another.

I'm very grateful for the help and support we had; it was truly precious. But still, that time was very hard. I felt that I lost everything I had, the stable and comfortable life that was taken for granted before. And the worst part of that situation was that I couldn't be with all the people I love. Men aren't allowed to leave the country during the war, so they have to stay. It was so hard to see women with kids. Almost each of them had several or even more than three kids. Many of them were less than six months old. Women's eyes were desperate. We all rushed to leave our homes because the situation was horrible. We didn't understand how fast the invaders might reach our cities.

Now I'm back home. I spent a wonderful summer with my family. Of course, there were scary days, and there were thoughts about whether to leave again or not. But there were also great days when our soldiers did the impossible to bring our territories back. You can't imagine the atmosphere here in Ukraine when we receive good news! Maybe, this is the only way to make the nation stronger and to show the price of being home. Now, we all know that it takes only one second for life to be dramatically changed.

There have already been several missiles that hit the buildings next to my home. I came to see one of these houses with my own eyes to understand what the weapon managed to do with it. There used to be a small two-floor house before. Luckily nobody lived there. There were several shops on the first floor selling household goods. One night changed this house significantly. Coming closer to that place, I noticed more and more glass on the ground and less in the windows. The explosion was so intense that it broke nearly every window in this district. And then I saw that house.

It impressed me so much that I stayed next to it for quite a long time. It seemed that a giant hungry creature came and bit a part of the building—the very middle of it. Imagine biting a watermelon and leaving a semicircle on the piece. The same was here. For a moment my fantasy drew a picture of that insatiable creature biting the house and everything inside of it.

That creature has already been doing this for 7 months now. I have a feeling that it is trying to eat our lives, our homes, our memories, beliefs, feelings, and souls. I am very grateful that lots of countries around the globe are helping us to get rid of this awful creature. I believe in us, in people who respect each other's rights and understand that life is priceless. I'm sure that soon with everybody's help this creature won't be able to keep stuffing itself with our destinies. It will have only one way out—to eat itself. When it happens, I'll start my stories as I used to: "The sun is shining and the birds are singing…"

There Is No Time for War

There is one family who came to my hometown. An 18-year-old boy brought his four brothers and sisters. He hoped to find shelter here. His mother died in his arms. They were on their way home when a bomb exploded near his mom's leg. Her last words were that she was okay. He cries every time he talks about that moment. He cannot understand why or what she died for. That boy did not know how to tell his brother and sisters what happened, but when he came back home alone no explanation was needed.

Igor

When everything started, I was abroad. I was safe. However, I wanted to go home, as never before. I clearly remember the moment when my husband woke me up in the middle of the night to tell me everything had started. I have never prayed so much. Not only that, but I have never read the news to such a degree. I did not cry. I just did not understand what was going on. How can it be possible in the middle of Europe in the 21st century?

A week ago, we were talking to my parents. They were a little bit scared that war was possible. I just laughed. Ukraine has no time for war, I thought. There are so many problems to solve.

Now, all dreams and wishes are connected only with the war ending. It is a tragedy and has already broken so many lives.

A friend of mine works in Poland, but all her family had been living in a Ukrainian town far from Kherson. They were lucky enough to be evacuated at the very beginning of the invasion. Can you imagine? Her parents are both over 60. My friend's mom worked as a kindergarten teacher, and she loved that job. Her father had a small local business. They built a lovely house, which took a lot of money. They lost everything and had to flee to another country without knowing the language or how long they would be gone. Do you know what really surprised me when I spoke to them? They told me that, luckily, they lost only their house and job. Some people lost family, friends, and lives. After our conversation, I understood that this war highlighted what is really important. No goods or material things could be more valuable than human life.

Now, my friend's mom is learning a new language, and her dad has already found a job in Poland. So, even though their town is totally destroyed, including the kindergarten where her mother worked for twenty years, and almost all the people they knew have run away, they still dream of coming back and rebuilding their house.

I met Olga at the railway station. She and her two children were scared and had only one bag. The youngest cried that he wanted to go home. Olga tried to pretend that this was just a short trip, a journey, and they would return home in a few days. Her children probably understood what was going on, as the Polish railway station was overcrowded with Ukrainian people. A few hours before our meeting, they'd crossed the border.

Olga and her children spent three days in Ukraine. During that time, Olga turned on the news, and there was their flat. It was bombed. For two days, she cried and tried to make a plan. After that, she gathered all her bravery, took her boys with that one bag, and started to follow her new strategy. She always dreamed of visiting the USA, so why not go there? She had nowhere to come back to. I lost contact with her. I hope she finally finished her journey and found a safe place for her children.

A few weeks ago my friend, Anna, came from western Europe. She lives in Lviv, and since the beginning of the war she has stayed there. It was her first dose of Ukrainian reality. She was not bombed or held captive. However, when she heard the airplane crossing the sky over her she was terrified. Her hands started to shake.

I took an online lecture with a girl from the western part of Ukraine. It started to rain, and my teacher was scared. She took a minute to check if it was really raining. She thought that it could be the bullets.

Maybe all these stories are not that scary and, somehow, these people can be called lucky because they are safe and alive. However, there are millions of such stories. I am not sure how long it will take for them to stop being scared of rain and airplanes. So many homes have been destroyed, and people made to start over. This war has changed our children for sure. There were recommendations on how to talk to children about the invasion to make the facts less painful and traumatic for them. However, they understood everything. A lot of them have grown up too quickly because of this war.

There is one family who came to my hometown. An 18-year-old boy brought his four brothers and sisters. He hoped to find shelter here. His mother died in his arms. They were on their way home when a bomb exploded near his mom's leg. Her last words were that she was okay. He cries every time he talks about that moment. He cannot understand why or what she died for. That boy did not know how to tell his brother and sisters what happened, but when he came back home alone no explanation was needed. At that time, he had to take responsibility for the family. They had no relatives, as his mom was an orphan, and he did not want to talk about his father. So, the next day he took them and evacuated to a town in the western part of Ukraine. They had only documents. He even had to ask volunteers for a jacket.

Now they live in a dormitory. People try to help them with food and clothes. He cooks, checks homework, and takes care of his younger siblings. Sometimes, that boy helps other people who also come to that town because of the war. Government aid and donations help him greatly, so he tries to share with others. He described his previous home with a smile. It was a big house with a separate room for every child. In the backyard, there was a lovely garden with trees. That was the reason why they did not evacuate at the very beginning. His mother thought this war would be finished in a few days and they could stop hiding and go back to their garden.

I met another girl from the eastern part of Ukraine. She is a mom of two incredible children. The youngest was only 4 months old when they had to run away. Her husband was a volunteer at the hottest spot of the war. He went missing a few weeks ago. There is no information, no messages from him. Every single day my friend is waiting for a signal from her husband. Her brother-in-law died in this war, so it would be too much for their family to know that one more member is not alive. So that girl tries to persuade herself that he is safe and looks for a reason why he did not call. Hope helps her deal with the challenges that everyday life brings her. She is alone with two toddlers in Germany, but at least they have hope.

She is not alone in that hope. So many people believe that their loved ones who are fighting for independence will come back home alive as a hero and, finally, the war will be over.

For now, after all those months of the war, life in Ukraine has become so confusing: one friend is getting married, and another's husband died. While someone opens a new business, others lose their jobs because companies go bankrupt. On the western side, there are dances, laughter, and celebrations. While on the eastern side, people are learning how to live in a new reality without loved ones or some parts of the body.

On the Internet, pictures of happy people are mixed with the news and videos from the eastern part of Ukraine.

People try to live a normal life and return to reality, despite how cruel it can be. No one believes this war will end in a few days or weeks. However, everyone tries their best to help finish it as soon as possible. The level of patriotism is higher than ever before. The Ukrainian language has become so popular and conscious Ukrainians try to use it in everyday life, even if they are from the eastern part of Ukraine where Russian is spoken. There are a lot of volunteers who continue to help. There is such respect for the Ukrainian Armed Forces. They learn so quickly and really fight for independence. They do an incredible job and, thanks to the help of friends worldwide, can protect their homes.

This war created a lot of tragedy but also highlighted all the kindness and bravery of people. It was incredible how everyone opened their hearts and homes to strangers, shared food, clothes, and donated what they could. Some did their everyday duties, despite the danger of bombs. Drivers, backers, workers of the shops, and many-many others never stopped working. Thanks to them, people had the possibility to take care of themselves.

This war connected people, especially after the Covid pandemic, but let it be over now.

Then, finally, Ukraine can live without checking the news from the front and start rebuilding into the prosperous and incredible country it deserves to be.

Silent Victims

Feldman Ecopark, a private Zoo on the outskirts of Kharkiv, took the heaviest blow. The first animal victims perished on February 24. About 100 animals were killed in total, including bison, apes, and kangaroos.

Roman Cherevko

As soon as the first missiles and projectiles had exploded across Ukrainian cities on February 24, 2022, hundreds of thousands of people were forced to leave their homes and seek refuge abroad—or at least in those regions of the country that seemed safer. And many of them had their dogs, cats, and other pets with them.

We all have seen the pictures, like the viral *Wall Street Journal* photo of a girl with disabled dogs fleeing Irpin near Kyiv. "We had no doubts in this regard," said 20-year-old Stasia. "Even if the dogs panicked and got stubborn, I would still drag them out."

Or you might have seen the story of 61-year-old Ihor, who walked 150 kilometers from Mariupol with his dog Zhuzha when the city was under siege.

"I'd Rather Die Than Leave My Animals"

Sadly, not every story has a happy ending. Some animals couldn't survive the long road to safety. Others were abandoned by their owners who had run in panic or perhaps thought they would come back in a day or two. These animals often died of hunger or were killed by bombs.

But even in these difficult situations, there are people willing to sacrifice their safety and comfort for other living beings. Dozens of volunteers continue to stay in dangerous areas and occupied cities to help animals left in apartment buildings and in the streets.

UAnimals, the major Ukrainian animal rights initiative, keeps in touch with these volunteers and delivers pet food where possible or transfers money if they are in the occupied territories.

Thanks to the volunteers, some animals were able to reunite with their owners.

UAnimals tells the story of Milka, a cat from Mariupol. When shelling started during the evacuation, the cat owner's mother, who was carrying the animal, had a heart attack. The carrier fell to the ground and opened, and the frightened cat ran away. But Mariupol's volunteers found Milka and helped evacuate her to her family.

Another Mariupol cat, Limosha, ran away when a projectile hit his house. The owners couldn't find him and had to evacuate without him. After wandering for a long time, the cat came back to his destroyed house, where volunteers discovered him and returned him to his family.

Animal shelters also found themselves in a difficult situation, since it's not always possible to evacuate large numbers of animals or to feed them.

Sirius is the largest shelter in Ukraine, located in Fedorivka, north of Kyiv. There are more than 3,000 animals under their care. It was blocked and then occupied for over a month. When food ran out, the shelter's owner, Oleksandra Mezinova, traveled through nearby villages to buy cereals, potatoes, or anything at all.

When Borodianka, a town near Kyiv, was liberated, 222 dogs were found dead in a local shelter. They had died of hunger and thirst, and activists blame the woman responsible for the shelter, who refused to help and left the dogs in closed cages.

By contrast, Andrea Cisternino, a 63-year-old Italian and former photographer who founded the Rifugio shelter near Kyiv, said he would rather die than leave his animals. His shelter is home to over 400 animals including dogs, cats, and horses, as well as farm animals whom he saved from butchery.

78-year-old Asia Serpinska, who takes care of more than 700 dogs and cats in Hostomel, also couldn't imagine leaving her animals. Sixteen dogs in the shelter were killed by the Russian artillery. Ms. Serpinska says the Red Cross denied her any help, so her family had to make dangerous trips to bring food, water, a power generator, and gasoline.

Shelling and Lost Revenue: The Plight of Zoos

Ukrainian zoos attracted some public attention after the start of the full-scale invasion, but wider media coverage is certainly desirable in this case, because the zoos are in dire need of help from the public.

Feldman Ecopark, a private Zoo on the outskirts of Kharkiv, took the heaviest blow. The first animal victims perished on February 24. About 100 animals were killed in total, including bison, apes, and kangaroos. Many animals were evacuated, but UAnimals accuses the zoo's owner of being reluctant to cooperate, which cost lives.

The large Zoo in downtown Kharkiv is threatened, too, since the city is constantly being attacked by Russian troops. The same is true of the Zoo in Mykolaiv, another front-line city.

In addition to enemy fire, another problem is the loss of income. Before the war, the Mykolaiv Zoo was especially popular during the summer season. Many tourists coming to seaside resorts like Koblevo did one-day tours to Mykolaiv to visit the zoo. Today, there are no visitors and thus no resources to buy foodstuff for animals or do infrastructure repairs. The zoo's only hope is in volunteers and donations.

The situation at other zoos throughout Ukraine is not much better, since domestic tourism and the leisure industry are at record lows.

The Center for Rescue of Wild Animals, based in Chubynske near Kyiv, does great work in getting zoo inhabitants, particularly large predators, to safety. The center's owner, Natalia Popova, evacuates animals with the help of volunteers and the military. Most recently, they have been rescuing animals from Donetsk Oblast. The Zoo in Poznań, Poland, is helping Natalia to get animals to places where they will have decent care, organizing their transfer to Spain, France, and South Africa. As of August, 200 animals were sent abroad and another 100 found shelter in Western Ukraine.

Serious Impacts on Animal Husbandry

Back in May, Taras Vysotsky, Deputy Minister of Agrarian Policy and Food, said Ukraine had lost 10–15% of its livestock. This included farms near the front line as well as in the occupied territories.

It's hard to estimate the exact number of animals killed, but there were cases where about a thousand animals died from a single missile attack: in one such case, on August 31, a Russian missile destroyed half of the 2,000 livestock animals at a farm in Zaporizhzhia Oblast.

Volodymyr Aliokhin, a farmer from the front-line village of Pavlivka in Donetsk Oblast, was able to evacuate 400 sheep after losing over a hundred animals in a mortar shelling. On July 19, about 50 cows burned alive at a dairy farm near Bakhmut, also in Donetsk Oblast. Six days earlier, 400 pigs had been affected when a missile hit Odesa Oblast. In addition to barley and sunflower stockpiles being lost, 30 pigs were destroyed in Dnipropetrovsk Oblast in June. Dozens of cows were killed in late March at a farm in Kharkiv Oblast. Also in March, dozens of ostriches died at a farm in Yasnohorodka, near Kyiv.

When Lukashivka, a village near Chernihiv, had been liberated after 21 days of occupation, 160 dead animals were discovered at a local farm. "We saw horrible things. Cows died together with their newborn calves…these savages were killing animals just for fun; they organized safaris to hunt them. Then they took the best pieces of meat to eat, and the rest was just left lying there," said Hryhoriy Tkachenko, the farm's owner.

But the enemy has kept shelling farms near the Russian border even after these territories were liberated. On August 28, Russians attacked a herd of cattle in Semenivka, Chernihiv Oblast. On September 18, they killed about a hundred pigs and a horse in Volfyne, Sumy Oblast.

Numerous equestrian facilities were affected by the war, too. In March, a stable in Hostomel burned down with the horses inside. When a fire started in Borodianka, the stable's owner managed to open the paddocks and let the horses run free. A donkey who was in the stable died in the fire, while the horses wandered through the adjacent fields for the next 45 days. Two of them died, but the rest were saved after the region was liberated. Another equestrian club near Kyiv, Rodeo in Horenka, lost over 10 horses. And in June, all the horses burned alive in a stable in Metiolkine, near Sievierodonetsk. In this case, activists once again blamed the owner, a Russian supporter, who refused to evacuate the horses.

Another problem stressed by owners of both farms and horse stables is that grazing near the front line and in the recently de-occupied territories is dangerous due to the mines left in the fields. Thus, they have to rely more on fodder, which means additional costs.

Endangered Wildlife

When I first heard the news about the Russian troops in the Chornobyl Exclusion Zone on February 24, I immediately remembered my trip there in 2016. After passing the checkpoint, the first thing we saw was a herd of Przewalski's horses. Far from being a lifeless wasteland, the zone was officially named a nature reserve in 2016, and these rare wild horses are among its most treasured inhabitants. Thus, any fighting puts the animals in serious danger.

The same is true of other protected areas like Ichnia National Nature Park in Chernihiv Oblast, where the retreating Russian military left behind many mines, which could cause forest fires.

Fires are raging along the front line, as can be seen on satellite images, which means many animals are dying or forced to leave their natural habitats. Moreover, the enemy often prevents firefighters from doing their work, which further exacerbates the situation.

Askania-Nova, Europe's largest steppe reserve, is another object of concern. Founded in the nineteenth century, it is home to many rare animals, including the above-mentioned Przewalski's horses. Today the reserve, located in the left-bank part of Kherson Oblast, is under occupation. Just like the Mykolaiv Zoo, it was a popular summer tourist destination. Now the employees who stay in the reserve can only rely on donations to help the animals survive the winter.

It Will Take Decades to Restore the Dolphin Population

The true scale of the damage to sea life will only be revealed after the war ends, but as early as April, Ivan Rusiev, an ecologist who works at Tuzly Lagoons National Nature Park in Odesa Oblast, started sounding the alarm due to dead dolphins found on the Black Sea coast. In June, he said 3,000 dolphins had already died. In August, his estimate was 5,000, but he stresses that the actual numbers could be much higher since only some bodies are washed ashore while others sink to the bottom.

The ecologist says that not only are he and his colleagues discovering many more dead dolphins than during previous years, but also that the bodies have no traces of poachers' fishing nets, meaning the cause of death is something different.

Rusiev explains that sonar used by Russian warships and submarines damages the dolphin's inner ear, and the animal loses the ability to echolocate. As a result, it can't find food or avoid obstacles, its immunity weakens, and it becomes susceptible to viruses.

The ecologist says dead dolphins have also been found in other Black Sea countries, including Romania, Bulgaria, and Turkey. Moreover, Turkish and Romanian scientists have confirmed that most of the dolphins had inner ear damage. Dead animals were observed in Crimea and Russia, too. Russians say the cause of death is infection, but Rusiev stresses the possible link to Russian sonar.

It will take decades to restore the dolphin population, says Rusiev, and the drop in this population will create an imbalance in the entire marine ecosystem.

Who Will Pay?

While it's not 1939, when Brits, at the beginning of World War II, killed their pets in fear of food shortages, animal casualties are still horrifying and our furry friends are still largely unprotected.

Even if some die due to the negligence of those responsible for them, this negligence is caused by the pressures of war. Most often, animals are dying either in random firings, as accidental casualties when the target is humans, in targeted attacks on farms as part of the "hunger terror," or as a result of pure indifference to all life, as in the case of the sea activity or the intrusions on nature reserves.

In all these cases, the culprit is the aggressor. Although we don't have exact numbers yet, it is likely that more animals than humans have died in this war, probably in the hundreds of thousands.

This is a blow not only to the flora of Ukraine, but also to the biosphere of the entire planet.

And there are neither international conventions to protect them nor reparations due to them.

My Inner Battle

This war differs significantly from the tales our elders told us about the conflicts they witnessed in the 20th century. Nowadays, you won't often see your adversary holding a gun to your head; instead, artillery, drones, and aircraft are used to fight most wars.

David

Beginning of the crisis

Despite the fact that many individuals in western nations had already begun talking about a potential conflict between Russia and Ukraine, I believed that it was unlikely to occur before Russia took any more significant action on the eastern side of Ukraine (Luhansk and Donetsk). I believed that the issue would remain unresolved between the Ukraine and Russia unless a miracle occurred and Zelenskyy and Putin reached an amicable resolution.

In the week after Putin declared that Russia would take the Ukrainian areas of Luhansk and Donetsk, I came to the terrible realization that the unresolved dispute was likely to swiftly worsen and turn into war. The myth that Ukrainians are insanely brave proved to be true. Only a small number of people made the hasty decision to flee the country, but the majority opted to remain with their countrymen. Nearly all of my relatives are still present in Ukraine as of today. They do have a place to go, therefore the reason is not that they lack options but rather that they are a unique breed of people. For instance, my 81-year-old grandma never considered leaving Ukraine. However, the majority of my friends and family are located in western and central Ukraine where the calm has been partially maintained.

My inner battle

When the conflict began, I was going through an extremely difficult time in my life. I barely had a year left to finish college, but as time passed, my sense of patriotism grew stronger and harder to suppress. Despite the fact that I know nothing about guns or warfare, I felt it was my obligation to support my nation in some manner. But, in the end, common sense prevailed and I understood that there was nothing I could do until my nation called and ordered me to go fight for it.

I continued to study for my examinations and fulfill my regular responsibilities, while also being on call to assist my family and friends when necessary. Even though a war was going on, I attempted to maintain as much composure as I could and made the decision that our opponent would not have an affect on my work, mental health, or physical well-being. So far, nothing has changed. I am grateful to God for giving my family and me the courage to carry on while maintaining our most precious possessions. Although some are material items, many of these possessions are primarily spiritual. Our house is still intact and undamaged, and I hope that will remain the case until the awful crisis in Ukraine comes to an end.

I also ask God to protect any innocent people who are out there in the middle of a conflict. I don't just mean civilians, of course. Many others, some even younger than I am, are carrying weapons and attempting to defend our nation. I sincerely hope that all of these heroes will survive to the war's end.

Story of my close friend

I often think about a friend of mine who is a little older than I am. He was a very modest individual who primarily performed manual labor. He didn't enjoy braggadocio, acting tough, or being haughty. After completing an army course where he learned how to wield weapons, he volunteered and enlisted to fight for his nation when the war started. Happily, he is still there and still living. He assured me that the conflict is not at all what a person would truly think. It differs significantly from the tales our elders told us about the conflicts they witnessed in the 20th century. Nowadays, you won't often see your adversary holding a gun to your head; instead, artillery, drones, and aircraft are used to fight most wars. That's what he told me, and the information truly astounded me. It just proved to me that I really have no ability to help my country in terms of fighting on the battlefield. I also heard a story about a neighbor who enlisted in the military and was deployed to the east of the country. He tragically perished when a missile struck the truck in which he and his fellow volunteers were traveling.

Atmosphere at the moment

More and more people are leaving our country as the battle intensifies. That is understandable, and I think that all women, children, and elders should leave and save their lives until better times come. On the streets, there are both peaceful and chaotic moments. I believe it to be the same as what is said about every warring nation. As people become accustomed to sirens, they stop yelling, hiding, and running. However, this does not imply that they wish to continue leading that life; rather, they are merely adjusting to the present and hoping for a better future. I still have hope because I believe there will be brighter days ahead and that this war won't go forever.

My day is easier since I am busy with tests and academic obligations which prevent me from having many free moments to think negatively. That's what makes my life simpler, but not everyone will agree. My granny finds it difficult to get through the day without worrying about how our people are being oppressed by a Russian invasion. And that's not even the worst case. The mother of my friend who volunteered and went to the battlefields of Ukraine is in a really bad mental condition. She is living in fear every day because she doesn't know if her son is well. And what makes this tragedy even more tragic is the fact that she is not the only mother who spends every day waiting in anxiety for her son to return home. I try not to pay attention to figures and numbers because they have such a profound effect on me, but I'm pretty sure thousands have already died in this six-month-old battle. And the only thing we can do is pray that those figures don't go up.

Who is right?

Now, the hardest question for everyone at the moment; Who is right in this gruesome political war that doesn't benefit anyone? I will stay as neutral as I can, and be as objective as possible. As the old saying here goes, an argument always needs two. So I think you can never say one side is 100% right, and the other is 100% wrong. That doesn't even make sense mathematically.

The key talking points are Donetsk and Luhansk. According to Ukraine, these areas should be part of Ukraine but Russia disagrees. So, I have a fairly straightforward question for our enemy; Even if we lift our hands from these territories, will that be enough for you? I, personally, highly doubt that to be true. Their main goal is not conquering those territories. They want much more than that and that's the main problem. We would be left sitting and pleading with Putin not to annex 80% of our area if Ukraine were to capitulate and hand over all of its weapons to Russia. The Russians ventured much farther into our land than what they initially claimed belongs to them, which serves as evidence of this.

However, the fact that neither of the two opposing sides is willing to understand the other is what is keeping the war from ending. While Ukrainians are concentrating on explaining why Russians should be viewed as villains who spreads death throughout our country, Russians are focusing on proving how Ukrainians are fascists terrorizing Russian civilians. Do not misunderstand me; I do not believe that Russia and Ukraine should become best friends overnight, but peace cannot be achieved if both sides concentrate on the negative aspects of the other.

Life after the war

What kind of life will we have following this crisis that has afflicted our nation is the most crucial way? In my opinion, it will take a long time to recover from these dreadful tragedies. However, rebirth is always preferable to annihilation. Therefore, the sooner our nation achieves peace, the sooner we may resume our pleasant lives. Actually, the very fact that the conflict is over will make our people happier. Therefore, achieving peace should be our people's top priority in order to avoid escalating the conflict to global levels. Our people and Russians would both agree with me. I'm a perpetual optimist, so I'll always think well of our future. Whatever occurs, I don't believe anything will harm our nation or our people. We are tenacious and tough. We don't let our guard down easily.

Perspective of the others

We don't want to be perceived as aggressors, though. We are the group fighting to protect our communities, institutions, and country in this conflict. By no means did we intend to incite them into a conflict; that would be absurd. Who would wish to endanger their own nation in order to start a conflict? The fact that many who support Russia think we are the ones who started this war and that Russia is merely defending itself bothers me the most. They believe we should just sit here and take it. There are those who still believe that Russia is merely protecting itself from Ukraine despite the fact that our nation is under attack from many different directions. Does the defending side always demolish the infrastructure of the adjacent nation, including its airports, buildings, and the homes of tens of thousands of innocent people? You cannot make sense of this argument. Russia is waging an invasion against us in an effort to seize control. My nation's only options are to defend itself or give up.

Our side of the story

I've already said why giving up is not an option. Ukrainians are aware of who they are dealing with and know that our capitulation would significantly threaten our existence. So we have to go for a second option, and that's defending ourselves until the dawn rises. In my honest opinion, we, as a nation, should maintain our integrity until the aggressors understand that only an agreement, not force, will prevail. Putin needs to understand this and tone down his arrogant remarks. The conversations between Putin and Zelenskyy should advance with humility, respect, and reason. So let's work on these issues and bring peace and happiness to both Russia and Ukraine. Nobody wants their infrastructure, morals, or character to be destroyed. Both sides are losing, and it will be like that until the war comes to an end.

There are two potential causes for the end: one favorable and one disastrous. As I am optimistic, I will firstly describe the positive scenario. That scenario represents the miracle that I mentioned in the opening of this article. Actually, establishing peace seems like an overstatement given the current scenario. But in reality, it's not really a miracle; all that's required is for both leaders to sit down and realize that after the conflict both our nations and peoples will be significantly weaker. After reaching that conclusion, their egos and intransigence should give way to their fear of such an outcome, and a compromise will emerge as a route out of this pandemonium.

The second scenario, which I'm sure nobody wants, is that both presidents put their egos first and use every tool at their disposal to win this conflict. That spells catastrophe for both nations. When resources run out the conflict will finish, leaving the country without its population, infrastructure, money, and other essential components for its continued existence. What makes this situation worse is that the nation that triumphs will have a very bitter victory. Whichever nation emerges as the stronger will ultimately turn out to be a very resource-constrained nation on the point of extinction.

Given that, I believe we can all agree that we would like the first scenario to occur as quickly as possible, before the second scenario is proven to be true and it is too late.

Wake Up

My black sweatshirt, black boots, black pants, and jacket, became my whole. The dust of the parking lot soaked into my skin and fabric. It flew around, inhaled by neighbors, dogs, and cats; it slowly enveloped cars in a thin film of dirt. Everywhere you went, it was with you, whether it was the small room with the crumbling wooden bench and bags where old people, including my grandmother

Mariia Lytvynchuk

From that night on, I could hear the sound of the dragonflies better. It was as if they were haunting me, urging me not to give up. They were something that I heard but couldn't see, couldn't touch, and I was unlikely to find. Where were they? I didn't know myself. I chased after the uncanny, trying to find the desirable. And while I searched, all I could do was write prose sitting on a wooden station bench, waiting for the familiar, the dangerous—what my soul found passionate…

A half-gray, half-blue, incomprehensible canvas gazed over my head, illuminated by a single streetlamp that I hadn't noticed before. The light was blurring my eyes as if I were only used to the watery lens that had enveloped me earlier. For months, my condition and everything around me had been difficult to describe. It was like I could still draw what was in front of my eyes as well as who was around and what I heard (not always), but normal human voices were like white noise to me, so why were dragonflies so melodious…?

I guessed the white noise was my main problem, which made it difficult for me to build a harmonious relationship with my family. When I was around my mother and sister, it was as if I was in a huge vacuum where I heard only indistinguishable sounds of emptiness. My body became light while my soul gained weight, like methane sinking into an abyss with no end in sight. It doesn't matter if it's a fight, a casual conversation, or a sit-down with an aura of love. I usually tried to keep the same feeling, driving myself into the noise…

I was told to write honestly; so be it. There would be no flowery confit, no love, and no tenderness in this story. Unfortunately, when it came to my family, that feeling was foreign and unexplored by me…

Our bonds became physically closer the night I began to hear the dragonflies, when that change from darkness to a Gothic winter morning was interrupted. We were to be awakened soon for school by an annoying alarm clock, but at 4:55 a.m., the gloom forever remained gloomy.

The dark clouds cut into my eyes. The sky was covered in semi-blackness. Neither the night light nor its intermediaries, whose twinkling was visible every night, illuminated the townspeople's way on this at-first quiet night. The frosty canvas, whose crimson-swamp-colored mantle was pierced underneath the muted moonlight, was impenetrable.

The nightmares sunk into a half-sleep. They bubbled in my cold body, which shuddered at the fleeting touch of the fresh, icy sheet on which my wounded hands lay.

The outside world forced an awakening. An indecipherable sound echoed in the distance of the city, muffled by miles and the tightly closed windows.

Breathlessness froze me. The sense of acute anxiety of awakening mingled with the barren joy of a passing dream.

No sooner had I sunk into another dream than there was another muffled explosion. The sounds were distant, but clear and shuddering.

However, neither reflection on the cause of the sudden noise that managed to wake half the city, nor anxiety, nor fear, were the reasons for the diligent beating of my heart. Thoughts were. And only them. Fictional scenarios swept over me as if a stormy wave greedily raked up every living thing and carried me into the depths of my heart, which was full of untouched treasures that no one could reach.

Blindness seemed to become my savior. Ears, on the other hand, were my nemesis. After two explosions, it was clear that shells of terrifying, destructive forces were flying at the city.

"But they could fly into my house, too… That would be so… beautiful…"

That thought alone made a smile cover my face, which flashed orange over and over again.

"Lying on the snow-white bed, she twisted from one side to the other, her legs entwined. She slowly, gently ran her fingertips over her stiffened wrist, counting the scars. The anticipation of death filled her being with a thrill of unearthly pleasure.

"Finally, her pleas for death were heard. The messenger from heaven was more tangible than God himself. A projectile flew into the room, its weight and speed shattering the sturdy windows into tiny shards, and the seemingly long, complex, and endless thing ceased to exist in the blink of an eye.

"In the pitch blackness, everything in the world ceased to tremble, and the last debris fell to the shattered floor, beside which already lay the wounded body of the girl whose heart was struck by one of the shards. Her blood mingled with the product of a squeak, which became the savior of the tormented soul."

Scenes of this kind haunted me all morning. This kind of bad thinking was not understood by my family and acquaintances, but it seemed beautiful and passionate to me...

My passion was a witness to the boundless human thirst for self-torture that helped to flood the shores of hope. While spending time in my illusions, corralling myself in my dusty corner each day, I liked to imagine myself as a character in a tragedy and found a kind of solace in it. In these fragments, I was carried along with my life in a fabulous cradle that swung so vertiginously that I felt like I was in the whirlpool of a sea rushing out of the depths and into the cosmic abyss. The sensation of my own death made me feel alive.

And then there was another explosion. The deafening sounds continued to prevent the city from sinking into the night and me, from drowning in my depths. After I stopped writing scenarios of my own death in my head, I tried to sleep again. However, the quiet moment was disrupted by the sudden messages that began to appear on my phone screen every second.

From that moment on, every house in my country was in turmoil and panic. The windows were lit up as if the houses were festooned with Christmas lights. People whose dreams were interrupted began to flee the city because of the news, which everyone learned in their own way.

Not being able to sleep for a long time, I spun in my crib as I imagined my friends, one by one, leave the city at an astonishing rate. In time, my yawn equaled the folding of another's suitcase. I felt like I had drunk a warm glass of milk. It spread inside my body, the liquid penetrating every crevice, the lactose soothing and harmonizing my cells; and though it was not the first time I had drunk it, on previous occasions the comforting warmth of the liquid could not overcome my nervous thirst. And yet, circumstances changed. The disaccharide had mingled with the ashes of the war and had taken on the property of healing my soul. And yet, was the revival of my eternally-dead inner world worth all the deaths I wanted to live?

However, the inexplicable equanimity that befell me did not befall others, including my family. At 6:30 a.m., the phone rang, for which I was ready. Remaining motionless, I listened to my mother's footsteps, who had awakened agitated and was still quite sleepy. Imagining the scene behind the wall made me feel like I was in a movie. I enjoyed it and prayed that the tranquility would continue to reign in my room, but that phone call spoiled everything.

The reason for my cold-bloodedness was crystal clear: the long agony of my anxious, creative being became human. My world had been destroyed, and the parts of me that lived in it would never be restored.

The dusky sky was heating the atmosphere of a wounded winter morning. My mother went hastily to wake my grandmother from her dead sleep. I didn't see it, but I could imagine my mother nervously waking my grandmother with the anxious words, "The war has begun."

It was hard to tell what emotions surrounded me with those words, but for some reason, I was at once making fun of and disturbed by my mother's excitement, which my sister soon picked up on as well.

In the words of my mother, my grandmother only waved her hand and replied: "You think it's all a dream. A long dream."

It was interesting to observe the old woman's disbelief about her possible death from the war because she had already experienced it in her early childhood. Wasn't that enough, after all?

My grandmother slept in the far room, which was wrapped up in other rooms and balconies, so the explosions were not audible there at all. However, even if a land mine had exploded in front of my grandmother, she would not have heard it. She was old and deaf. Frankly, she was hard to live with at that time, and we didn't get along. And sometimes I wondered why I felt that way about her. Why couldn't I say the words of love?

For years, I searched inside myself, longing to find the answer to that question. And soon I had an epiphany. It was as if I was trying with all my soul to be as cold-blooded as possible, knowing that my blood was not long-lived. Knowing that a person was about to leave me and that the lost souls of my neighbors awaited with the people I loved tore out pieces of my heart and drove me to deep despair. For this, the solution was clear as day: love no one.

Sometimes I felt a deep sense of guilt; sometimes it hurt so much to lie to myself that I didn't know what to do.

However, I had already decided this pain would be nothing compared to what awaited me in the future. Although, sometimes I was subjected to the deepest doubts…

I was raised by my grandmother and mother. For eighteen years, we had lived side by side, and for me, the word family meant the four of us and no one else. I remembered those moments from when I was very young. I felt like a lush dandelion that had just blossomed. And who knew that, like the flower, I would soon lose the seeds of happiness to the gusting winds of war.

My grandmother's love for me was enormous. She always stroked my hair with a happy smile on her face because she understood my peculiarity, which she also shared. I remembered how Julia and I always played with our dear grandmother while my mother was busy; I remembered how she baked delicious pies and her special pizza. Thinking back on those moments, my tears flowed and my emotions blended into a tangle of yarn. Flax grew from the root of sadness.

At precisely 7:00 a.m., the first siren sounded. Its hum sounded to the bone and awakened panic. The loudness of its frequencies came even through the windows. Its roar was specially recorded to cause panic and alarm, to make people move and make spontaneous decisions. And so it was with us. We hastily began to pack our bags to the sound of alarms.

However, for some reason, that alarm seemed so unique and beautiful to me. My creative, broken nature could not leave this moment an empty alarm in my life. In an episode of tragedy, I wanted to emphasize it with notes of sadness and confusion, knowing that our dame was not able to go somewhere.

Under anxious alarms, I sat down in my chair and touched the keys of my beautiful piano. Horror mingled with the hazy melody, and I felt as if I were filming a movie, enveloped in a hazy canvas of unreality. At that moment, I found solace in the tragedy. I had driven myself into the illusions of the world as the chaos was going on outside. How damaged was my mind for seeking calm?

Later, I realized self-defense was the culprit.

The first few days were monotonous. The phone was always in hand, the TV was always on, and the clothes that everyone wore since that first morning became an integral part of the body. It was as if, without this pile of threads, we could perish, as if one minute to change our clothes could cost a life. For in those days, no one knew the plans of the sinister.

Every three hours were indicative of the previous. My sister and I sat in the spacious living room the entire time, watching death through the screen, watching our lives change in front of our eyes. Afterward, a siren sounded. The horn would change the sequence of what was planned, and all that was left was to put on our jackets, put on our shoes, go down the stairs, and go outside.

At that moment, I remained as calm as ever, and only a little excitement brought a smile to my face. It was like a game to me, and life in it was worthless. Walking out of the house was like getting to the hottest spot on a level with maximum danger. And yet, for some reason, I felt as if death would not reach me. After all, it had already become clear to me that only the lucky died. I was not blessed with luck; I would not die.

I remember how brightly the sun was shining in those hours. Those frowning clouds that I thought the gunpowder trails would haunt had vanished. Why did they do that? Why did they leave us with nothing but attempts at clear skies? Nature and the universe had made it clear to us that we must deal with it by ourselves. To be in suspense, and with the next warning signal, to go out.

Oh, that sky! How beautifully it dazzled my eyes at the sound of the terrifying siren. The songs of the first swallows mingled with the frequencies of extraneous sound.

And with the first steps onto the cold pavement, I breathed in the mean flow of the February wind and squinted as I enjoyed the hymn of death.

My black sweatshirt, black boots, black pants, and jacket, became my whole. The dust of the parking lot soaked into my skin and fabric. It flew around, inhaled by neighbors, dogs, and cats; it slowly enveloped cars in a thin film of dirt. Everywhere you went, it was with you, whether it was the small room with the crumbling wooden bench and bags where old people, including my grandmother, sat; or the empty nooks of the parking maze where I left my footprints. The deafening silence was filled with my music, which carried frequencies to the high ceilings in barely audible echoes of sadness.

After a week of this routine, we finally decided to move out of a city that resembled a bonfire in which, as in Kotlyarevsky, the enemy roasted.

With difficulty, my mother managed to get us bus tickets to Lviv. Even though free evacuation trains were running at the time, we didn't dare take them. The panic of the situation awakened everyone, old and young, and with their small children and dogs, they rushed to the train station in the very center of Kyiv. In the peak hours, all the space was occupied. All the people filled the space and destroyed the laws of physics by not diffusing.

We saw it all through the TV screens. Those trains ran every twenty minutes, and a huge crowd gathered around those cars. Everyone was pushing and shouting and jumping on the train like crazy. Everyone was ready to stand in cramped quarters for days just to get away from the peak of the war. They stomped on each other, not afraid to kill each other; they jumped onto the already moving train, completely losing their minds. It was as if everyone had become insane and lost their humanity. Everyone turned on that stupid instinct of self-preservation…

Our departure was late at night. There was a curfew in the city, so when the sun went down, all the streets were completely empty. Only a couple of cars slipped in front of the eyes of stranded witnesses.

Alarmed, we tried to call a cab, which at this hour was a rarity. It was considered great luck to find a car that cost ten times as much as it did in peacetime. With each call, we were followed by an endless ringing tone and then it dropped. Finally, we were able to get through, and a hired cab was at our home shortly afterward.

Throwing, as I first thought, one last look at my house, we hit the road.

“Won’t we get shot like deserters at this time of day?” Mom said curiously, turning to the driver.

“It’s only happened three times so far, but I’m not sure. They’ve put up a lot of roadblocks now, so they mostly either stop on the spot or already check at the roadblock,” the man replied calmly.

"Aren't you afraid to drive at such an unsafe time?" I asked, surprised.

"It doesn't matter. Traffic is up a lot right now. I make as much a day now as I used to make a month. What's the point of me being alive and not being able to feed my family?"

At that, there was an awkward silence in the cabin, and only the furry lump I'd been stroking made loud meowing noises.

"Meow meow, meow meow, meow," he shouted in a voice not his own, tearing at his ligaments. Something was pent up in him. He could feel the sky's darkness. He knew what was going to happen in the next second.

A huge fluffy scarlet cloud appeared in the blink of an eye and shrouded the entire sky in the orange hue of fire. The silhouette reminded me of a mushroom. A huge, huge mushroom. And then there was the loud, shuddering sound of an explosion.

Everyone screamed in fear and surprise. The explosion seemed so close. It was shocking. In fact, it happened about ten kilometers away from us, which was relatively far, but the sight was so amazing that I thought I was right in front of the theater's main stage.

Still, it didn't last long. After a couple of minutes, we found ourselves at the station where our bus was supposed to be waiting for us. However, the entire perimeter was covered in darkness. The windows in the huge building, which had burned like bright fire in my memories, now only reflected the full moon that shone so brightly against the black tones. Neither the light of the moon nor the streetlights told us the way into this desolate place. Silence reigned. There were no people, no cars, no so-called bus that we were so ready for—no one. Just emptiness.

"Are you sure this is the right place?" the driver asked doubtfully, circling the building.

"Yes… I'm sure." My mother stretched out the words. I could hear the nervousness in her voice. The first notes of fear coursed from her chest to her throat. It enveloped her. Surprisingly, it enveloped me too.

"But there's nothing here," the man replied, confused.

"Mom, aren't we going anywhere? I want to go," my sister repeated nervously.

"You can go to the station and wait for the evacuation train. I think you can make it by morning," suggested the driver, stopping.

This suggestion caught us off guard. And after a five-second pause, a showdown ensued. My sister insisted on going to the train station and leaving. My grandmother began to ask my mother about her thoughts and plans, but my mom had no idea what to do next. I wanted to go back and wake up again in my own bed, in the city which had become my everything. My heart fluttered so excitedly at the risk of staying home.

Having expressed my firm reasoning, the decision was made in my favor. We went back inside.

And as soon as we opened the front door, as the familiar smell tickled my nostrils pleasantly, a message arrived for Mom. Our landing had been rescheduled. We were supposed to be at the same spot at 9:00 a.m. the next morning. So we were. That same day, we left.

The next evening, we were already in Lviv. I met a bunch of relatives I didn't even know I had. Who knew that the war would reveal to me my previously-hidden family tree? They, like the same petals, enveloped us in a warmth and kindness that I hadn't felt in so long. For a few moments, I felt the happiness that an ordinary person feels. I cast aside all my dreams and allowed myself to be in the sky of the fluffy clouds that hung over that tree.

The following days I spent with my new relatives. School was canceled, and I forgot about it in a day. Thoughts and plans completely left me and I just enjoyed the moment. I enjoyed walking around the village that was north of the city, enjoyed the delicious food that my great-aunt cooked for me, enjoyed the gusty wind while my feet were pedaling my bicycle, and enjoyed the children's laughter and my cousin's naivety and infantilism.

With amazement, I enjoyed life.

A month and a half later, a lull was declared in Kyiv and we returned. While all my friends continued to hide out in different countries, I stayed at home, hardly ever going outside. The change of scenery and stressful thoughts about the future rid me of all my nightmares and depressive thoughts. They seemed to disappear in an instant. Although, I think it was also influenced by the antidepressants that I had started taking the day before the war.

I was immersed in thinking about my future because it was the year of admission. All over the country, almost everyone I knew was preparing for the exam to continue their studies in the capital. However, this city was weighing on me. And though it was very close to me and I loved it very much, I understood that I could not stay in it any longer.

A break from school and complete immersion in myself helped me understand what I wanted to do: write. This was my vocation, this was what I was ready to spend hours on, this was where I could pour out my soul…

With that revelation, I decided to go abroad, and the next weeks were filled with searching for a country and an institution. My head was filled with nothing but that. I did not even notice how time flew by; I forgot about everything that was happening outside, and only the frequent sounds of sirens, which froze the city for a few hours, brought me back to reality.

After months of searching, the University of Canada responded to my email. And I, along with my sister, began preparations for admission.

At that time, the news of the war had reached the whole world, including Canada. There was a group of people who agreed to help us, and together, we began to raise money for our studies on another continent. The collection grew slowly, but after a while, we had the tickets in our hands and knew we were definitely going.

Still, just the tickets weren't enough. We had to get more. I made up different stories and posts. Also, one of the things I had to do was send a picture of us together for the website.

Then I went outside for the first time in a long time. The warm stream of rays covered me from head to toe. The frequent songs of birds covered my ears. My gaze fixed on the trees. It seemed it was yesterday that they were all naked, but now, they were dressed in lush spring foliage that swayed slightly in the light breeze. Everything had changed so quickly… I couldn't believe it. I just stood there, staring into the void, feeling my body begin to sweat under my black winter jacket.

If You Want to Help

The National Bank of Ukraine for Humanitarian Assistance

Special account of The National Bank of Ukraine for Humanitarian Assistance to Ukrainians Affected by Russia's Aggression. Money transferred to this account will be used by the Ministry of Social Policy:

- to provide food and shelter for refugees and citizens that have been displaced due to military conflict
- to provide clothing, shoes, and medicine for them
- to buy staple goods for the population
- to pay out one-off financial aid and to meet other essential needs of the population.

Resource: https://bank.gov.ua/en/news/all/natsionalniy-bank-vidkriv-rahunok-dlya-gumanitarnoyi-dopomogi-ukrayintsyam-postrajdalim-vid-rosiyskoyi-agresiyi

For USD remittances:

Beneficiary: Ministry of Social Policy of Ukraine

Beneficiary BIC: NBUA UA UX

Beneficiary address: 9 Instytutska St., Kyiv, 01601, Ukraine

Account number: 804790266

Bank Name: JP MORGAN CHASE BANK, New York

Beneficiary Bank BIC: CHASUS33

ABA 0210 0002 1

Beneficiary Bank address: 383 Madison Avenue, New York, NY 10017, USA

Purpose of payment: for ac 32302338301027

For EUR remittances:

Beneficiary: Ministry of Social Policy of Ukraine

IBAN DE85500000000050002137

Purpose of payment: for ac 32302338301027

Bank Name: DEUTSCHE BUNDESBANK, Frankfurt

Bank BIC: MARKDEFF

Bank Address: Wilhelm-Epstein-Strasse 14, 60431 Frankfurt Am Main, Germany

For GBP remittances:

Beneficiary / Recipient Name: Ministry of Social Policy of Ukraine

Account number: 80033041

IBAN GB52CHAS60924280033041

Beneficiary Address: 9 Instytutska St, Kyiv, 01601, Ukraine

Beneficiary Bank Name: JP MORGAN CHASE BANK NA, London

Beneficiary Bank BIC: CHASGB2L

SORT CODE: 60-92-42

Beneficiary Bank Address 125 London Wall, London EC2Y 5AJ, UK

Reference for crediting account: 32302338301027

The Global Ukraine Foundation

The Global Ukraine Foundation focused on creating a leading global community of, by, and for high-impact founders and investors who are committed to (re)build Ukraine across its financial, professional, and social spheres. The Global Ukraine Foundation is a U.S.-based donor-advised fund (501(c)(3) charity tax deductible project "Foundation for Ukraine" under CAF America.

ACH TRANSFER

Charities Aid Foundation America (CAFAmerica)

Account #: 226005698262

ABA Routing #: 054001204

Bank of America

2747 Duke Street

Alexandria, VA 22314

USA

WIRE TRANSFER

Charities Aid Foundation America (CAFAmerica)

Account #: 226005698262

Wire Routing #: 026009593

SWIFT: BOFAUS3N

Bank of America

2747 Duke Street

Alexandria, VA 22314

USA

Address: One World Trade Center, suite 8500, 285 Fulton street, NY, 10007, New York, USA.

Authors

Andrii Yankovskyi

Mariia Lytvynchuk

Marina Petrovska

Roman Bohdan

Roman Cherevko

Sofina Kateryna

Taras Romashchenko

Yana Rybak

Yuliia Tatarchuk

and others that wish to remain anonymous

Translations

Oksana Dymaretska

Editors

Cindy Draughon

Clare Jordan

Danny DeCillis

Dante Antonio

Gennifer Ulmen

Lily Sperber

Nismeta Kabilovic

Sarah Hawkins

Siera Schubach

Special thanks to Taras Romashchenko Ph.D

Associate Professor Department of Economics and International Economic Relations Institute of Economics and Law (Deputy Head) Bohdan Khmelnytsky National University of Cherkasy

Contacts: t_romaschenko@ukr.net & linkedin.com/in/taras-romashchenko

Made in the USA
Columbia, SC
07 December 2024

48384222R00157